YOU ARE HERE 2

YOU ARE HERE

2

A NEW APPROACH TO
SIGNAGE & WAYFINDING

First published and distributed by
viction:workshop ltd.

viction:ary™

viction:workshop ltd.
Unit C, 7/F, Seabright Plaza,
9–23 Shell Street,
North Point, Hong Kong
Url: www.victionary.com
Email: we@victionary.com

 @victionworkshop
 @victionworkshop
Bē @victionary
 @victionary

Edited and produced by viction:ary
Creative direction by Victor Cheung
Book design by viction:workshop ltd.
©2022 viction:workshop ltd.

ISBN 978-988-74629-5-8
Printed and bound in China

It is human nature to seek out clues and reference points in our surroundings to understand where we are and which way we are facing. We are constantly scanning our environment for landmarks and features in the landscape such as rivers, trees and distinctive buildings, to gain our bearings and to make sense of where we are.

The same is true in the built environment, we register features in the cityscape and we take notice of memorable points along the way — even sound can play a part in helping us to orientate. This intuitive process enables us to mind map our surroundings, often subconsciously.

We draw upon this natural urge to make sense of our world when designing signage systems. When we consider the wider orientation process, we can complement it with a layer of graphic and physical interventions to bring further coherence to a specific journey or place, establishing a sense of order and legibility. Wayfinding is the term we use when we combine natural reference points with signs to create holistic orientation systems.

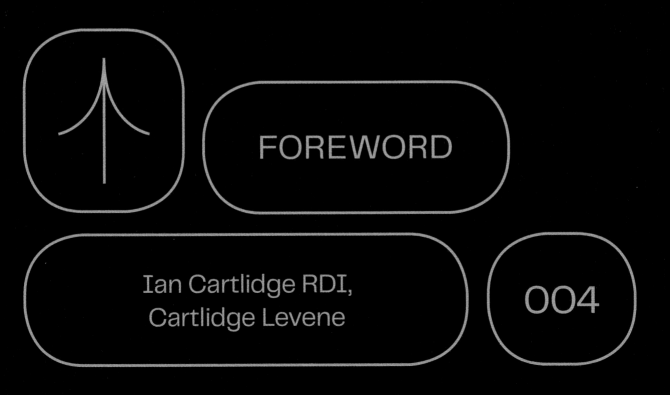

FOREWORD

Ian Cartlidge RDI,
Cartlidge Levene

004

A small number of well-placed signs, complimenting the natural wayfinding elements that exist around us, will be more effective than the introduction of a multitude of signs. As our surroundings become ever more crowded with information and messages, we begin to switch off and no longer read or trust what we are being told. A calmer, more considered approach is always welcome.

Similarly, poorly designed signs are often less effective than well-designed signs. Well-designed signs consider their locale and integrate with the rhythm and materiality of a building or streetscape. Signs are most powerful when thought of as an extension of architecture or landscape design, seamlessly merging physical and graphic interventions as one experience.

Today, digital mapping apps play an important role in how we navigate, instantly pinpointing our location and telling us how to get to where we are going. But it is wayfinding interventions in the physical world that create powerful emotional resonance — this is what we rely on to guide us through complex and sometimes confusing environments. Well-designed and carefully placed signs can be inspiring and uplifting, providing us with a reassuring helping hand as we traverse through our natural and built environments.

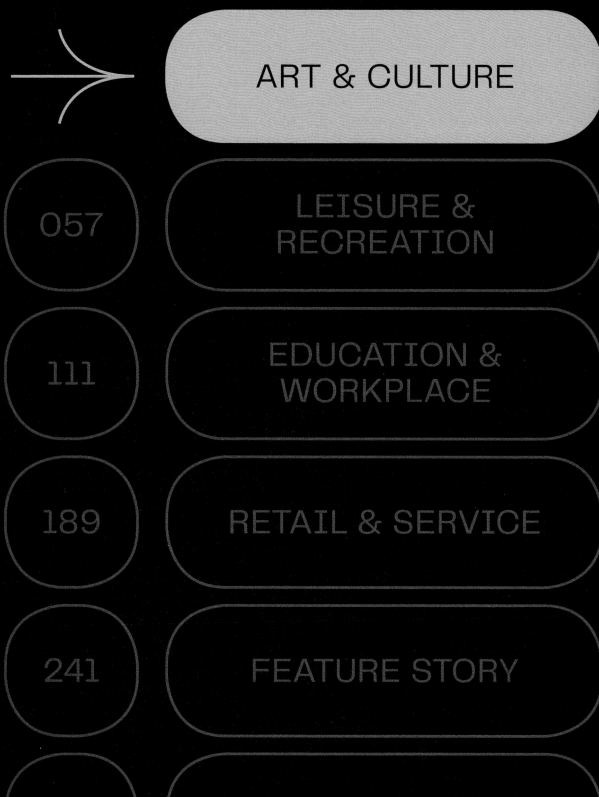

BRITAIN
(1500—1760)

52—58

V&A

DESIGN
dn&co

CLIENT
V&A

STRATEGY
allpointswest

dn&co was tasked with developing a comprehensive wayfinding system that could enable visitors to explore the exhibits with confidence and curiosity. The V&A wayfinding system had to live comfortably with the museum's rich collection, while sitting within Grade I listed surroundings. Made from tulipwood, dyed black and stripped from any extraneous colour except to highlight paid exhibitions, the signs conveyed a sense of quality and permanence, while acting as a beacon that lets visitors navigate the busy ground floor and keeping the permanent galleries free to explore.

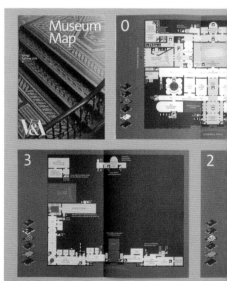

Musée d'Arts de Nantes

DESIGN
Cartlidge Levene

CLIENT
Nantes Métropole

PHOTOGRAPHY
Marcus Ginns

The Musée d'Arts de Nantes is one of France's largest fine art museums that displays works from the 13th century and beyond. Working closely with the museum and architects, Cartlidge Levene designed the museum's visual identity and wayfinding system with a clear objective to deliver a holistic approach to graphic design across all mediums. For signboards and maps, a chiselled, Futura-based font was cast into concrete and rendered into the walls or applied as raised lettering to timber surfaces. Key locations such as the chapel and the Cube were also marked with a small, raised motif in the museum's trademark magenta and yellow.

Collections 19ᵉ–20ᵉ
Cube ▨

Patio ▪

V&A Dundee

DESIGN
Cartlidge Levene

CLIENT
V&A Dundee

PHOTOGRAPHY
Marcus Ginns

V&A Dundee is Scotland's first dedicated design museum by architect Kengo Kuma. Cartlidge Levene was commissioned to create a wayfinding and signage system for the museum and its surrounding landscape along the River Tay. At the entrance, visitors are greeted by a large sculptural version of the iconic V&A logo sitting in the water, framing the museum. Heading into the atrium, level directory strips clip onto horizontal timber planks, while oak lettering and pictograms extend the timber language to the white-walled gallery level above. The reflections of the logo create an ever-changing mood, adding to the sense of arrival.

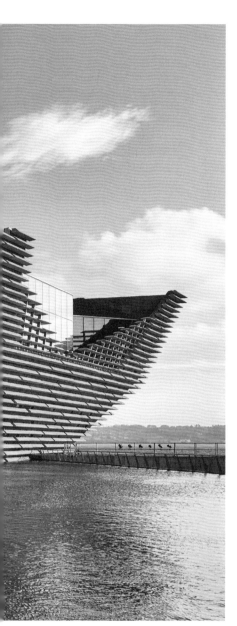

Robert Barr's Charitable T...

The Kennedy Charitable...

Evelyn Ferris Mudie Charit...

Thomson Learning Centre

Weston Studio

Royal Opera House — Open Up

DESIGN
Endpoint

CLIENT
Royal Opera House

PHOTOGRAPHY
Hufton+Crow
Photography

Ever since its 'Open Up' project in 2018, The Royal Opera House in London underwent a transformation into a daytime destination that welcomed a new audience and visitor journey. To enhance visitor experience, Endpoint developed a wayfinding solution that merged seamlessly with the sophisticated combination of wood veneer, stone marble and gold. Designed to be subtle but not hidden from plain sight, directions and signage were carefully placed and designed so as to not to appear intrusive with an elegant and refined font. A new set of donor boards were also erected to recognise project funders as part of its new naming strategy.

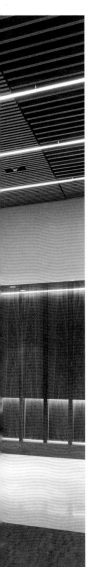

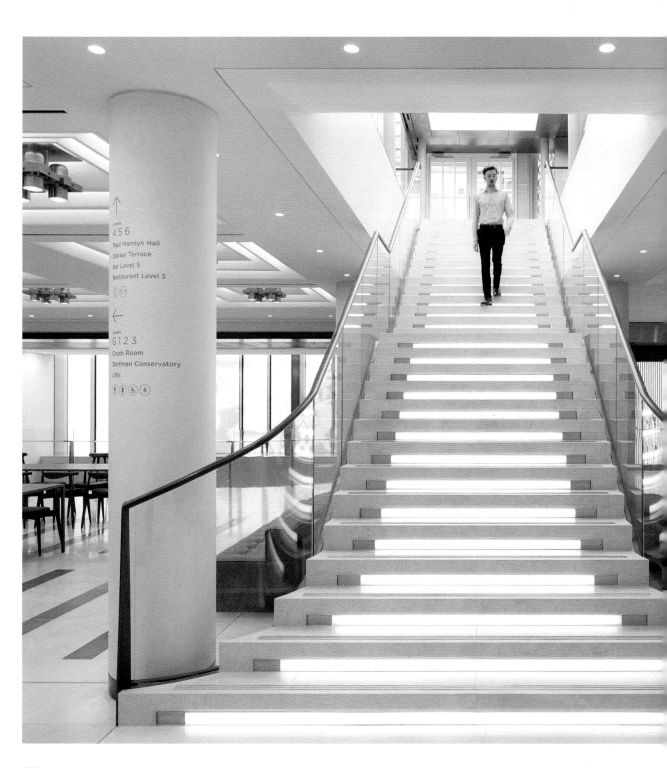

Levels
↑
4 5 6
Paul Hamlyn Hall
Davies Terrace
Bar Level 5
Restaurant Level 5

←
Levels
G 1 2 3
Crush Room
Dorfman Conservatory
Lifts

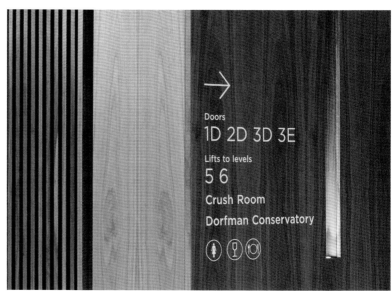

Doors
1D 2D 3D 3E

Lifts to levels
5 6

Crush Room

Dorfman Conservatory

THE ENTRANCE TO

THE ROYAL OPERA HOUSE

IS GENEROUSLY SUPPORTED BY

**THE MONUMENT TRUST
IN MEMORY OF
SIMON SAINSBURY**

2018

DAVIES
TERRACE

GENEROUSLY MADE POSSIBLE
BY DR GENEVIEVE DAVIES
AND FAMILY
2018

The Santa Fe Opera

DESIGN
Two Twelve

CLIENT
The Santa Fe Opera

After undergoing a renovation funded largely by donor contributions, the Santa Fe Opera contracted Two Twelve to design all-new signage recognising the Opera's benefactors. Combining modernity and inspiration from classical Greek art, the result was a timeless design that blended seamlessly into both the architecture and breathtaking local landscape. The signage included dark stone plaques with high-shine finishes that reflect the gorgeous scenery, while the back-of-house signage maintains visibility in low light, with peg letters that can be removed for the re-stuccoing of the facade.

CIBOLA
PLAZA

Gift of Betsey & Budd Knapp

The mythical kingdom of Cibola was part of
Native American legend, later incorporated
into Hispanic folklore. This plaza celebrates
Native American and Hispanic culture.

Shiga Museum of Art

DESIGN
UMA/design farm

CLIENT
Shiga Prefecture

INTERIOR DESIGN
graf

CERAMICS
NOTA&design

Surrounded by greenery and an idyllic view, the Shiga Museum of Art in 2021 underwent a renewal project and contracted UMA/design farm to develop a new visual identity and signage system that connected the museum and its surrounding plazas. With simplicity and legibility in mind, signage design was kept to a minimum, while outdoor signposts took the form of hollow cuboids stacked vertically, bearing the directions on its surfaces. The material for the three-dimensional signposts are created from Shigaraki ware, a type of traditional stoneware known and used in the local area since ancient times.

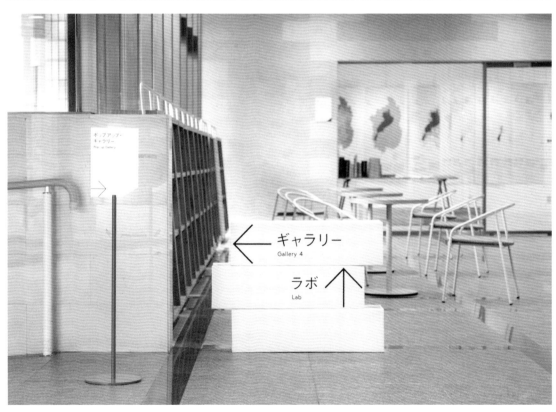

コールダーの庭
Calder Garden

ファミリールーム
Family Room

展示室 3
Gallery 3

3

XIXI LIVE Signage

DESIGN
702design

CLIENT
XIXI LIVE

XIXI LIVE is an experiential theatre scene that unleashes youth and creativity through the mutual stimulation of space, setting and the audience themselves. Taking inspiration from their unique composition, 702design incorporated an altered, almost mutated form of Chinese characters into the wayfinding of XIXI LIVE. By first disassembling, overlapping then fusing together the characters' radicals and sides, the end result is a new glyph that tells a story and gives a new meaning to the space that it represents. These glyphs may appear strange, but are ultimately recognisable to eyes that are familiar with the Chinese script.

Ticket Office
取票取

Man　Woman
男　女女

No Smoking
炆

Western Australia Art Museum

DESIGN
Studio Ongarato

CLIENT
Western Australia
Art Museum

ARCHITECTURE
Hassell + OMA

PHOTOGRAPHY
Peter Bennetts

The new Western Australian Museum designed by Hassell + OMA was conceived as an 'activated' museum. Large scale maps placed at strategic locations encourage visitors to curate their own journey across the galleries' collection of stories. The signage system harnesses a range of dynamic media, further prompting the wayfinding experience through sound and vision. The creative theme and conceptual notion of 'Sample' underpins the approach to signage forms and information through a range of dynamic signage display technology such as flip-dots, three-sided prisms and high-res LCD screens.

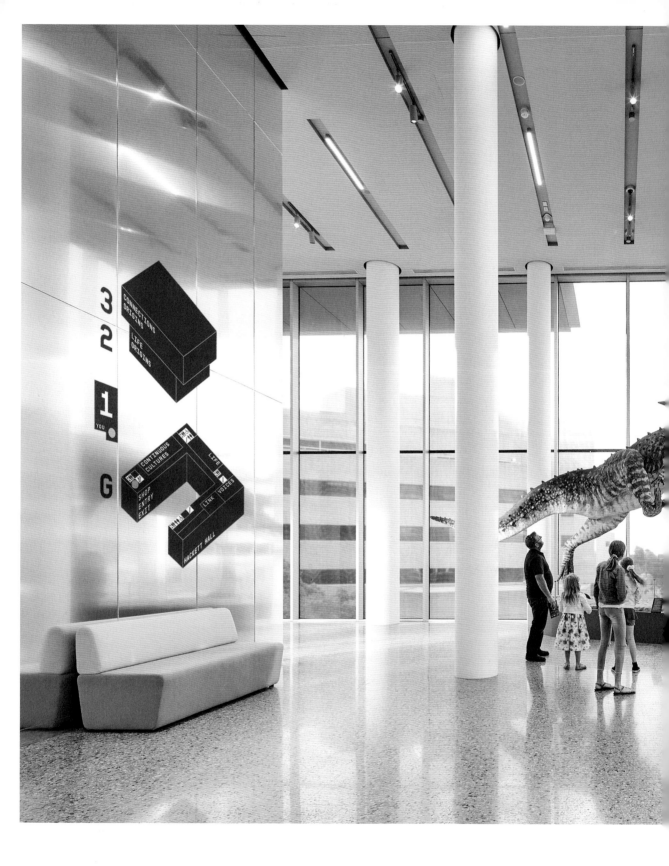

Art-zavod Platforma

DESIGN
Orchidea Agency

CLIENT
Art-zavod Platforma

PHOTOGRAPHY
Akim Karpach

Previously a silk factory, Art-zavod Platforma has been transformed into one of the biggest creative clusters in Ukraine, housing a cultural centre that holds a number of exhibitions, festivals, and other public events. In creating the wayfinding system for the premises, Orchidea Agency acknowledged the interchangeable nature of the event halls and rooms and created a flexible, dynamic sign system in the form of an orange metal grid that allows its contents to be modified and switched around when needed. To differentiate the Loft area from Co-working spaces, a different colour code was also used to identify the function of each building.

Fabrika 1830 Signage

DESIGN
Tuman studio

CLIENT
Fabrika 1830

Fabrika 1830 is a revitalised art quarter on the site of what used to be the Balashikha Cotton Spinning Factory. While the factory's authentic atmosphere has been preserved, the interior has been transformed into a cultural arts hub at the heart of Moscow. In developing its wayfinding system, Tuman studio based its design on the initial concepts of interwoven threads. In selecting the construction materials for signage, a long metal mesh grill references the texture of the fabric while protecting the contents from eroding, allowing the elements to be harmoniously combined with the environment and Fabrika's historical past.

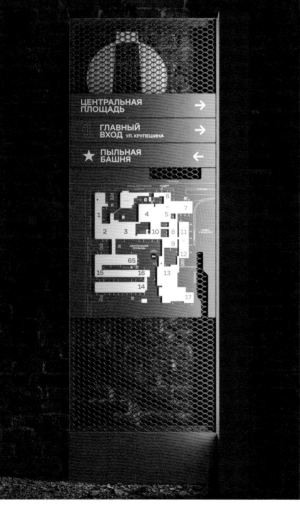

Squash 73

DESIGN
Mariela Mezquita

CLIENT
Squash 73

PHOTOGRAPHY
Camila Rodriguez

Squash 73 is a multidisciplinary, cultural space in what was once a squash club. The aim was to create a fresh and playful identity that spoke to a young audience about the creative possibilities within the place while keeping in mind its athletic roots. This was accomplished with dynamic graphic elements that come from the reinterpretation of old squash tactics diagrams. For the signage, the concepts of versatility and movement were interpreted in a three dimensional form where folded steel and wire were contorted to form various pictograms, creating an eye-catching and innovative way of navigating around the area.

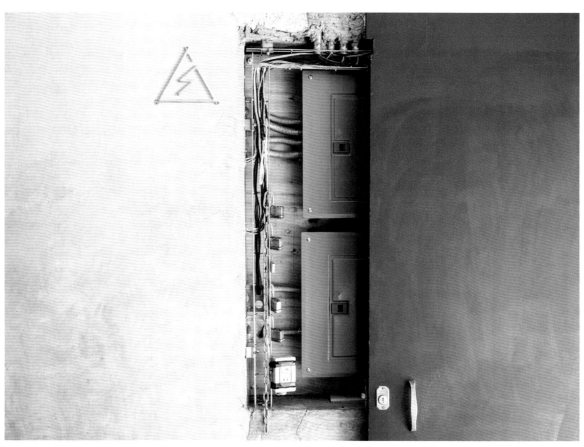
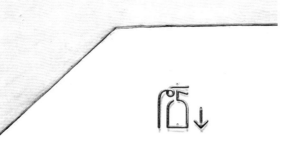

CHAT

DESIGN
Toby Ng Design

CLIENT
Centre for Heritage,
Arts and Textiles

Centre for Heritage, Arts and Textiles (CHAT) is a cultural arts centre located at The Mills in Hong Kong, focused on weaving together contemporary art, design, science, heritage, community and craftsmanship. Inspired from the fundamental structure of warps and wefts used in weaving textiles, CHAT's logo reflects its mission of interlacing different voices, disciplines and practices into a vibrant cultural tapestry. The logo also doubles as a hashtag to symbolise its contemporary relevance and groundbreaking innovation. The logo is integrated into a series of signage and environmental graphic applications that were also influenced from notions of weaving.

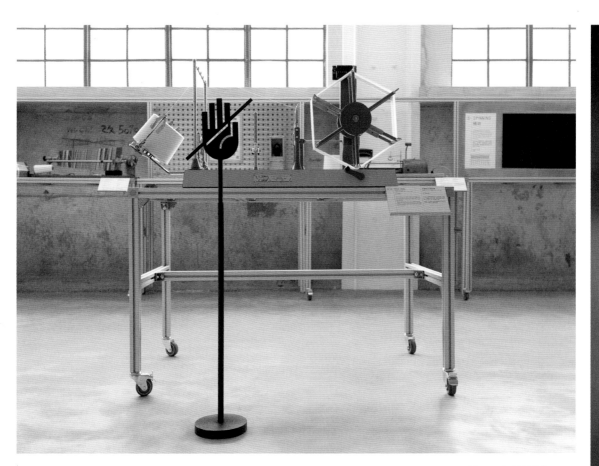

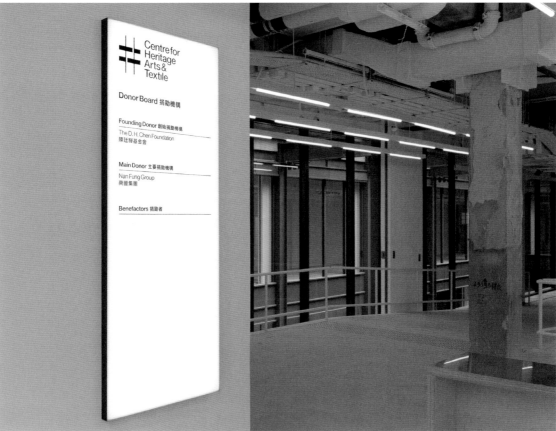

Centre for
Heritage
Arts &
Textile

Donor Board 捐助機構

Founding Donor 創始捐助機構
The D. H. Chen Foundation
陳廷驊基金會

Main Donor 主要捐助機構
Nan Fung Group
南豐集團

Benefactors 捐贈者

BOK Building

DESIGN
Smith & Diction

CLIENT
Scout Ltd.

SIGN FABRICATION
DNL-DSN

The BOK Building is a historic building that was previously a technical school, now spanning across an entire city block in Philadelphia. After undergoing a revitalisation project and transforming into a community of makers, artists, small businesses, and nonprofits, BOK needed a sign system that can grow with the community. From building maps to outdoor signage, each level was sorted into distinct geometrical patterns and colour codes that correspond to the directory. The flexible signage system can adapt to all kinds of new creative tenants and establishes the building's tone as a vibrant, diverse space.

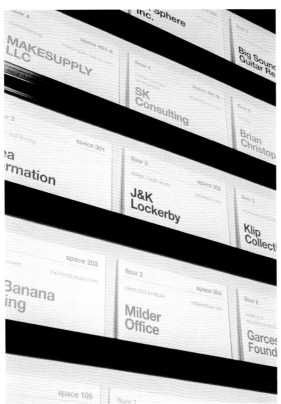

What are your main considerations when it comes to integrating signages with architecture, interiors or spatial design?

When working on a new space, we always pay attention to blend the signage into given space. Materials, sizes, interior design — all are very important. But it is behaviour analysis of users, that allows us to provide attractive and effective solutions for every building or space. When designing, we are not afraid to reach for all possible tools for message visualisation like a sheet of paper, pencil, felt-tip pen, paint, 3D printing or unusual execution materials. This approach allows us to develop creative solutions tailored to the diverse needs of our clients and spaces.

● Blank Studio

Always design for the context. Consider how the wayfinding reflects and represents the place it is located in.

Wayfinding is often one of the first touchpoints for people in an unfamiliar environment so it must reinforce a sense of place and align with either brand values when working in commercial environments, or reflect and work with local character, architecture, and the wider urban realm in cities. That comes through both the information that is included in wayfinding as well as the overall look and feel of any product — it needs to answer the question the user is asking of it to create a positive experience.

That's what is great about designing the systems we do — they support positive experiences and offer a better understanding of places through good design.

● Applied Information Group

Comprehensive design direction of branding, concept, typeface, colour, material texture, temperature, and atmosphere to create a unified impression across all design categories.

● artless Inc.

Architects plan, craftspeople build. However, what is the role of designers on a building site? They help people find their way. Wayfinding systems help people navigate in buildings or their surroundings. They resonate with identity, atmosphere and narrative. We all want to be informed about how we can get to where we need to go. And we all want to express who we essentially are.

● Sägenvier DesignKommunikation

It should be a comfortable design that does not interfere with architecture and blends into the space.

● AFFORDANCE inc.

Respecting the architecture and the space where we will implement the graphics.

● pfp, disseny

Legibility of text and adequacy of introduced style and materials. Also, a secret ingredient — a big idea that can help distinguish this particular space from any other!

● Studio Blisko

As a branding and design studio, we often approach signage as an extension of the visual identity. To us, signage should be able to bring together functionality with the experience of a brand. Our process begins from the moment we craft an identity, ensuring flexibility so that it may translate into applications such as signage whether it be through a connection to the logo or utilising other brand elements.

● Toby Ng Design

We always strive to integrate our work with the product conceptually, first and foremost. This philosophy applies to wayfinding in particular, which is exactly why we decided to let our signage spread further into the structure than a more classic approach would. Classic wayfinding icons are repurposed into playful, animated companions for new visitors venturing through the building. This in turn allows them to witness a gradual evolution of signage — from one that is purely functional to one that gives life to the space and celebrates its purpose.

● Studio Tumpić/Prenc

Each place's character and the ethos of the client organisation are at the centre of our design solutions.

● motasdesign

Our wayfinding process always starts with building a deep understanding of a project. We ask ourselves a lot of questions: what is the purpose of the space or building? How will people use it and move through it? What are a visitor's motivations and needs? Architecture itself is a form of wayfinding and we also need to consider the unconscious cues that our surroundings give us. Research and strategic thinking underpins everything we do. So whether we are working on wayfinding or place branding, understanding is the place to start in order to build a solid strategy.

Once we have clarity on that, our aim is to find a design language that fits the building and suits the ethos and aesthetic of the occupants — be they people, objects or both. A solution must be appropriate in both form and function and these are frequently in competition with one another. Often wayfinding needs to be noticeable, but not overpowering; it has to shout quietly. Challenges and constraints often guide our design solutions, bringing unexpected opportunities that inform architectural or material decisions.

Ultimately though, wayfinding must be consistent — whether that be in terms of material, content, or position. You have to be able to trust it; without that you're lost.

● dn&co

A wayfinding system must be well integrated with the architecture that it accompanies (similar materials, media formats adapted to the space, etc.). It also has to be functional — users must quickly get where they're heading. A well-designed visual information system should speak rather than scream. We have worked with both large, commercial (stadium, shopping centres) and public (schools, cultural institutions) facilities, and each requires a different approach. However, one thing remains unchanged — how crucial it is to understand who will use a given system and predict what problems they may have with it.

● UVMW

We ask ourselves a number of questions considering the integration of signages. The first is Quality of Location. Is this a key decision point where most building users need some navigation instructions? Does the location provide users with uninterrupted view of the sign in a position that is easy to see? Following that is Quality of Content. Have we got the naming right for destinations listed on signs and does it match what you provide people before they enter the building? More importantly, does it meet legibility requirements and creates an inclusive navigation message? Last is Quality of Object. Does the sign design fit with the architectural style, does it reflect the values and culture of the brand? Does it meet legibility requirements and creates an inclusive navigation message?

● Endpoint

Depending on the project, we like to take each commission in a different way. As our project involves a very important historical building, we wanted to integrate the signage with the architecture, being as respectful as possible with the existing details in the interior. The illustrations take a big role in modernising the signage, representing different activities held in each room and area, adding a human and distinct touch to the identity.

● Folch Studio

Our primary concern is the experience of people, in particular those who will live, work, or play in the place for which we are designing wayfinding systems. We think about the need for signs and other wayfinding tools to help people navigate and gather information they need. We also want people to feel connected and engaged by the places they are visiting. It is our job to marry this human experience and the dynamics of a building or place. Our wayfinding signage should feel natural, as though it really belongs to a place, part of the design expression of that place.

● Two Twelve

I always think about the route people will take when entering a space. It's useless to have a sign no one will see. I consider position, scale and legibility on signage to maximise its utility.

● Mariela Mezquita

Integration between signage and space is a very important topic and we usually dedicate a good part of our design process working on that. We believe that good integration with the architecture and interiors can enhance any signage system's efficiency and at the same time, the signage system itself will produce added value for the space. It's important to analyse carefully the space (from an early project stage if possible) and understand deeply how the architecture will shape the space and what kind of materials and colours will be used. We tend to have a tailor-made approach to the development of a signage system, so a deep understanding of the space will be a solid starting point for us to design something that can be efficient, well integrated and appealing to the user.

A signage system should have its own personality; it needs to be clear and affirmative and somehow be the consequence of a design concept that is defined for the project. But in the end, the signage system exists to make the space become more functional for the user, so integration and a good balance between both signage system's and space's personality are fundamental for a good overall experience.

● P 06 studio

When we work with wayfinding systems, we always take into consideration architecture of a space and the context in which it will exist, its authenticity. When it comes to signs integration, it is important to consider area specifics, find right placements and precise aesthetics. After all, since we work with communication, we must always think about how a person will interact with text and graphics in space, and help him/her to find a way around unfamiliar place, while not interfering with its identity.

● Tuman Studio

The main principle of integrating any navigation system into interior and facade solutions is to preserve visual accessibility. The navigation system should be firmly clear. At the centre of our projects is a person and his user experience. Through understanding the visitor's behaviour, we offer design solutions that are at the intersection of consumer marketing, architecture, urban studies, sociology and anthropology.

● ZOLOTOgroup

We first identify the character of the building or space. Then we analyse the materials and whether the architecture can support the wayfinding. If so, can the signaletics be more inclusive? We then consider the target groups and budget of the project. For every project and area, we will follow the flow of orientation, route guidance then goal confirmation, for several times if necessary.

● kong. funktion gestaltung

Signs are designed pieces of information, so flashy decorations may potentially interfere with the atmosphere. However, it is also important to appeal to the outside party, namely the users of the space. The key is to balance between the characteristics of both functional and eye-catching.

● 6D

I believe that the phase of the project that involves evaluating where in the architectural space to place the signage is important. For example, the functionality of the signage and the impression it gives users will vary significantly depending on whether the signage is placed on a wall or on the floor. I make an effort to achieve optimal placement of the signage for the building while evaluating the relationships between the space and the signage and between the users and the signage.

● Arata Takemoto Design Office Inc.

From a functional point of view, a successful wayfinding is one that enhances the understanding and experience of the space. Then, from the point of view of its expression, it must fit in a natural continuity with the architectural approach. In other words, it must blend in with the decor.

● byHAUS

While maintaining the balance of the entire space, we try to make the space more comfortable for users, and derive sign plans and colour plans from the shapes and materials that capture the characteristics of the architecture and interiors.

● UMA/design farm

Signage and architecture/interiors/spatial design are completely different in their essence. Architecture is a material thing we experience physically. Communication, by contrast, is a mental process; reading, seeing and wayfinding are actions. Text, arrows and colours are physical things, too, but they lack three-dimensionality, which makes them weaker than architecture. Integrating signage in a space, then, involves balancing out these differences: the weaker factor—the lettering—needs to be strengthened in relation to the manifest, architectural aspect.

The elements that support wayfinding need to be independent and self-assured, just like good furniture that matches and enriches a certain place's function, and therein lies the key: any intervention should suit each individual space precisely, enriching the architecture; it should be composed in relation with the architecture, but in such a way that equilibrium is maintained throughout and everything is brought together to form an inseparable whole.

● büro uebele visuel kommunikation

In order to express the concept of the 'place', I read the architecture and space. Signage is one of the elements of spatial design that people will always 'see', so I try to design signs that are not only functional and easy to understand, but also complement the meaning of the "place" that cannot be conveyed by spatial design alone.

● hokkyok

We consider wayfinding to be integrated into architecture and environment in two ways: (1) Integrated information — a carefully planned set of wayfinding elements offered at key points in the visitor journey. (2) integrated design — a design language that speaks about the environment and adds to the experience of place or building.

● Cartlidge Levene

In my opinion, the most important thing to factor in is the "identity of the space". Considering the function of the wayfinding system is necessary of course, but to contribute to the identity of a space is equally, if not more important. As such, I try to make a signage plan suitable for both the architecture and the space.

● ujidesign

There are many ways to integrate a wayfinding project into the built environment. However, it is a fact that combining strategic thinking from all disciplines from the early stages of the project is the right way to achieve better outcomes. The collaborative work with architects, landscapers, light designers, among others, provides more natural interventions in the spaces. Moreover, combine form and function, making the signage and wayfinding system more intuitive, logical and coherent with the architectural concept.

● Illustre Ideia Design

While it is important for signage to harmonise with non-signage elements, it is even more important that it not be too buried in the space. In other words, it is important not to seek the basis of the signage design too much outside of the signage. The goal is to be autonomous as a design.

● STUDY LLC.

Namiki Square

DESIGN
ujidesign

CLIENT
Fukuoka City

ARCHITECTURE
Yamashita Sekkei Inc.

CONSTRUCTION
Revive Co., Ltd.

PHOTOGRAPHY
Yashiro photo office

Namiki Square is a cultural complex that houses a multi-purpose hall, auditorium, municipal library annex and citizen's square. With the lack of wall partitions within the atrium, the pillars are designed to be visible even from a distance, reaching the ceiling and marked with large pictograms depicting the facilities on each floor. The flat pillars, as well as the rest of the sign system are also characterised by a distinctive zigzag pattern which references the same motif from the traditional Ayasugi crest of the region, forming the unique identity of Namiki Square.

2F

中小練習室　会議室
託児室　情報発信

トイレ　学習室

多機能トイレ　なでしこルーム
（学習ミーティング）

1F

なみきホール　貸出書庫

ひまわりひろば　キッズルーム

管理事務室　大練習室

トイレ　予約確認
サービスコーナー

多機能トイレ

Taga Town Central Community Learning Center — TAGA Yui no Mori

DESIGN
UMA/design farm

CLIENT
Taga Town

ARCHITECTURE
onishimaki +
hyakudayuki
architects / o+h

Built with locally-sourced timber from Taga town in Shiga Prefecture, TAGA Yui no Mori is a Central Community Learning Centre offering a homey community space with multipurpose rooms, event halls and workshop spaces. With an open-plan design and light interior, the pouring in of sunlight enhances the warmth of wood in the architectural design. With ligneous material as its central theme, the signage system was designed to meld into the interior with wood-compatible colours such as white and black. Small touches are seen in the rounded pictograms and font, which complement the interior's friendly and inviting atmosphere.

中会議室

和室1

中会議室

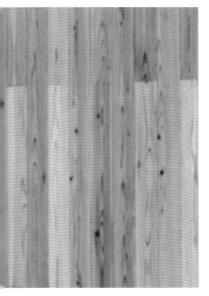

杉の子第2作業所
杉の子第2作業所

大会議室

Paracelsus Pool and Wellness centre

DESIGN
büro uebele visuelle kommunikation

CLIENT
Stadtgemeinde Salzburg — KKTB, Stadt Salzburg Immobilien GmbH

ARCHITECTURE
Berger+Parkkinen

PHOTOGRAPHY
Kurt Heuvens

TYPEFACES
GT America

Centred at the heart of Salzburg, Germany, the Paracelsus Pool and Wellness Centre was built to encourage locals to improve their health and find joy in swimming in its facilities, all while enjoying the magnificent view of the rooftops in the old city skyline. To guide pool-goers around the facility's pools, sauna and wellness centre, large, white three-dimensional letters float across the walls, arranged in rhythmic wave patterns as if gently in motion, echoing the central theme of tidal motions and referencing the building's architectural showpiece: the stunning, undulating roof that overarches the main pool.

Lonza Arena

DESIGN
kong. funktion
gestaltung, superbüro

CLIENT
Frutiger AG

ARCHITECTURE
rollimarchini architekten,
Scheitlin Syfrig

PHOTOGRAPHY
kong. funktion
gestaltung,
Simon von Gunten

FONT
binnenland

Despite its impressive size, the ice sports and event hall Lonza Arena in Visp was designed to blend in with the surroundings with transparent facades. With a capacity of up to 5,000 people, a legible and straighforward wayfinding system was needed to navigate the expansive space. As a solution, oversized, illuminated letters made from acrylic glass were installed from the ceiling as striking sector indicators. The original font "FRAC Lonza" is also used as a complement to the design language while reinforcing the Arena's spatial effect and function as a sports facility when viewed from the outside.

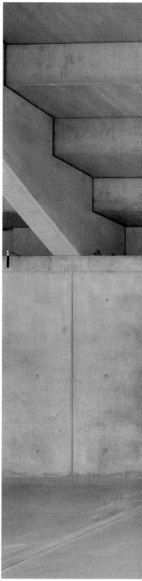

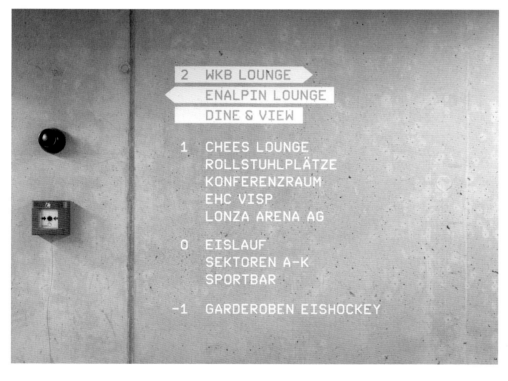

SEKTOREN D-K
SPORTBAR
GARDEROBE EISLAUF

2 WKB LOUNGE
ENALPIN LOUNGE
DINE & VIEW

1 CHEES LOUNGE
ROLLSTUHLPLÄTZE
KONFERENZRAUM
EHC VISP
LONZA ARENA AG

0 EISLAUF
SEKTOREN A-K
SPORTBAR

-1 GARDEROBEN EISHOCKEY

Stade de la Tuilière

DESIGN
kong. funktion
gestaltung

CLIENT & ARCHITECTURE
:mlzd, Sollberger
Bögli architectes

PHOTOGRAPHY
Ariel Huber, Simon
von Gunten

FONT
binnenland

Stade de la Tuilière is a football stadium located in the outskirts of Lausanne, Switzerland with a strong emphasis on function and structure. In tandem with the stadium's architectural design, a wayfinding system with a reduced visual language was also implemented. With a confined site area, the corners of the stadium are folded inward to connect the stadium square to the surrounding areas. Using the typeface "Formale Grotesque", the plain letters fold around the building as sector markings corresponding to the unfolded stadium corners, all to ensure that architecture and signage exist in a radically simple symbiosis.

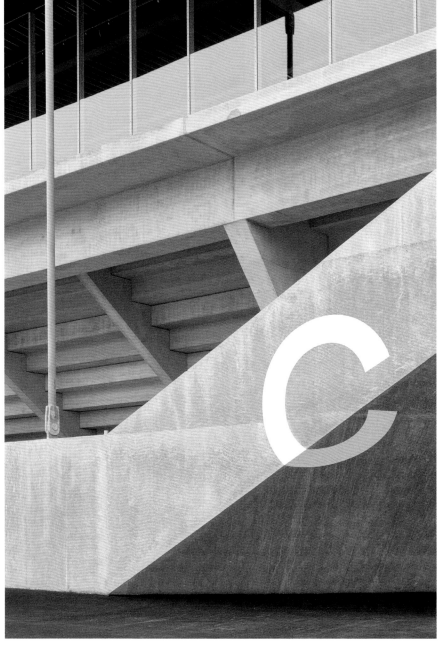

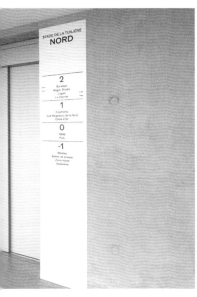

Memphis River Parks Partnership

DESIGN
Champions Design

CLIENT
Memphis River Parks
Partnership

SIGNAGE
Andrew Freeman

PHOTOGRAPHY
Bob Bayne
Photography
(Signage)

To welcome locals back into the newly renovated Memphis River Parks, Champions Design developed a new identity and signage system for a previously fragmented public property in Mississippi, United States. To connect the scattered locations, a new map was first drawn to determine the parameters and key locations along the riverfront. Then, Champions worked alongside afreeman design to create a series of arched, eye-catching signboards for every landmark. The sign is also decorated with a bold, legible font while specific landmarks also include a coloured plate that corresponds to the colour on the map.

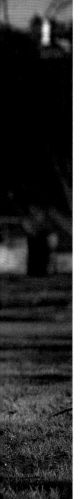

Casa Les Punxes

DESIGN
Folch Studio

CLIENT
Casa Les Punxes

INTERIOR DESIGN
Circular Studio

PHOTOGRAPHY
Aramis León

ILLUSTRATIONS
Josep Puy

Casa Les Punxes is a collaborative workspace based in Barcelona that takes co-working to the next level with a range of cultural programmes for personal wellbeing. Located in an iconic heritage building that mixes both antique architecture with modern elements, Casa Les Punxes features a welcoming identity that echoes with its dynamic environment. As navigation around the many individual rooms and facilities, signboards are accented with a classic and sophisticated font that complements the vintage exterior of the building, while signs for special rooms and spaces are accompanied by cheery and intuitive illustrations that make sense of its function.

COMMUNITY

MEETING ROOM

PRIVATE ROOM

PHONE BOOTHS

FLEX ROOM

COFFEE BREAK

FIX ROOM

EVENTS

MANDATORY USE
OF FACE MASK IN
THE COMMON AREAS.

USO DE MASCARILLA
OBLIGATORIO EN
LAS ZONAS COMUNES.

→

Private
Office 4

Private
Office 5

ÁREA RESTRINGIDA.
POR FAVOR NO ENTRAR.

Cloud

Office

Lobby

9 PEOPLE

IMUM CAPACITY
FORO MÁXIMO

Zen
Room

SE DO NOT LEAN
ER THE EDGE.

VOR NO ASOMARSE.

	YOU ARE HERE
A	ACCESS
R	RECEPTION
K	KIOSK
P	PLANTS
WC	BATHROOM
E	ELEVATORS
S	STAIRS

Fix
Room 2

→

Meeting
Room

Private
Offices 2-3

←

Flex
Room

Flex
Room

Storage
Room

Cloud

	YOU ARE HERE
M1	MEETING ROOM 1
M2	MEETING ROOM 2
M3	MEETING ROOM 3
M4	MEETING ROOM 4
M5	MEETING ROOM 5
M6	MEETING ROOM 6
G	GALLERY
W	WELLNESS ROOM
C	CANTINA
WC	BATHROOM
E	ELEVATORS

Office

FÖRENA

DESIGN
byHAUS

CLIENT
Groupe Skyspa inc.

ARCHITECTURE
LEM Gestion, Blouin
Tardif Architectes

Conceived from the wellness rituals of Icelandic, Germanic and Russian traditions, FÖRENA is a concept spa resort that resides in the tranquil foothills of Mont–Saint–Bruno, Canada with facilities such as thermotherapy, massotherapy and other aesthetic treatments. To express the spa's ethereal and mystical nature, byHAUS enhanced FÖRENA's wayfinding system with a unique typeface that explores contrasting themes of hot/cold, full/empty, shown in the thickness of each stroke, or through the solids and voids that make up the whole. The iconographic system respects the same scheme without lacking in functionality, with minimal lines that guide guests around the spa in an elegant, subtle way.

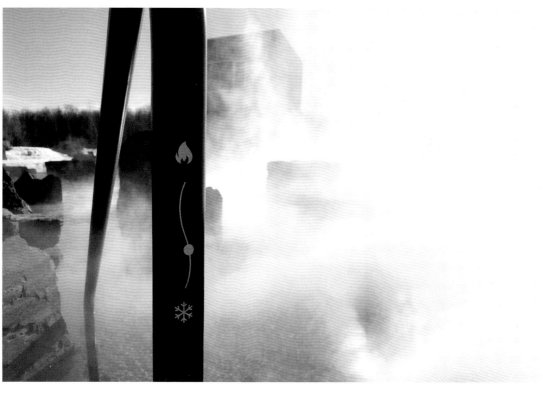

ÉTAGE
EXCLUSIF
AUX
SOINS

*Exclusive
floor
to body
treatment*

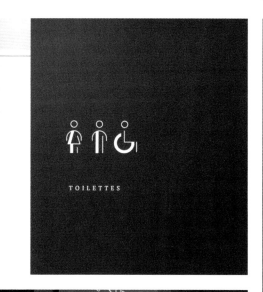

TOILETTES

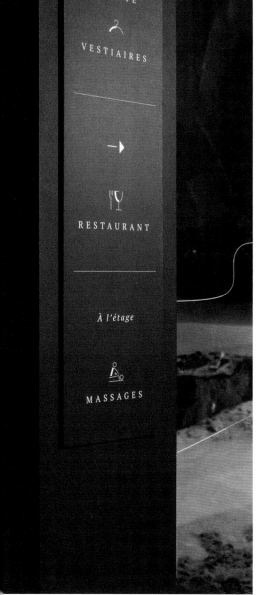

VESTIAIRES

RESTAURANT

À l'étage

MASSAGES

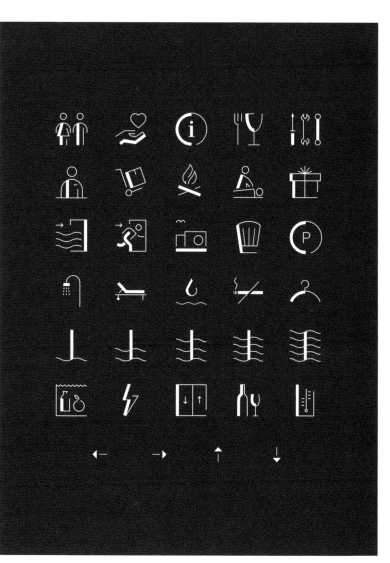

VESTIAIRE
FEMMES

SOLO SAUNA tune

DESIGN
STUDY LLC.

CLIENT
tune Inc.

INTERIOR DESIGN
Aki Hamada
Architects Inc.

PHOTOGRAPHY
Nacasa & Partners
Inc.

Nestled in the quaint neighbourhood of Kagurazaka, SOLO SAUNA tune is a Finnish-style sauna with private, individual rooms. Considering the sauna's location that is surrounded by temples and shrines, traditional Japanese lanterns and curtains were installed to enhance the tranquil atmosphere. Directions were replaced with pictograms in order to create a straighforward and legible wayfinding system that informs guests even in the sauna's dim lighting. Icons and room numbers were also designed with the same elements as the crest-inspired logo, which establishes a sense of unity with the interior.

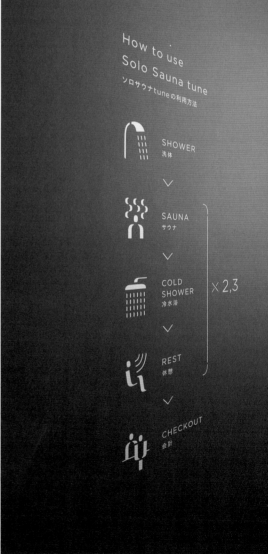

SHOWER
洗体

SAUNA
サウナ

COLD SHOWER
冷水浴

REST
休憩

CHECKOUT
会計

ROOM

1

ROOM

2

ROOM

3

Pula–Pola City Pools

DESIGN
Studio Tumpić/Prenc

CLIENT
Pula Sport

The underlying concept of using a line as the core graphic element for the wayfinding system for Pula–Pola City Pools was inspired by the conversations between Studio Tumpić/Prenc and professional swimmers, who explained how lines at the bottom of the pool act as guides towards their goal. With the same notion in mind, the signage on the cobalt blue walls are characterised by a long, continuous symbol of a wave accompanied by a set of self-explanatory pictograms. The wayfinding system was designed not only to be functional by helping poolgoers navigate around the facilities, but to also give life to the space.

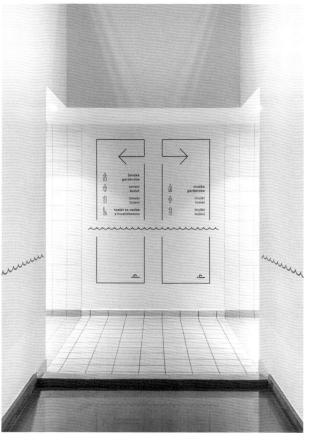

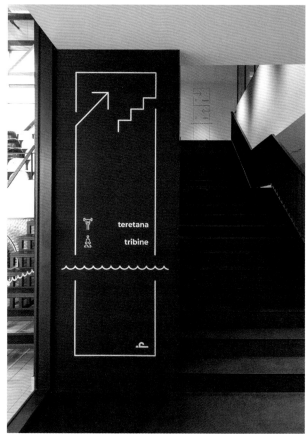

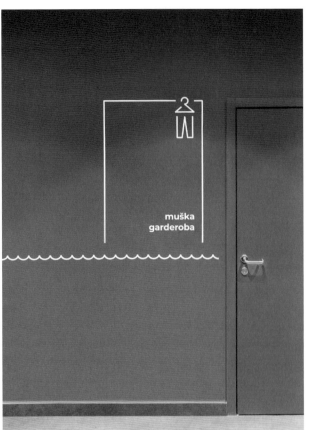

muška
garderoba

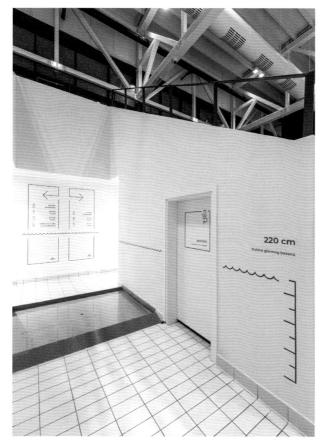

Dreifachturnhalle Wettingen

DESIGN
kong. funktion
gestaltung

CLIENT
Departement
Finanzen und
Ressourcen,
Immobilien Aargau

ARCHITECTURE
:mlzd

PHOTOGRAPHY
Ariel Huber

The Kantonsschule sports complex Dreifachturnhalle was built underground so as to not obstruct the view of a historical Cistercian monastery. Sunken large windows supply the gyms with daylight. The halls are characterised by a straightforward design: linear, fine white lines are used solely on the first floor, seen in the numbered markings of the walls, directions and the appearance of the handrails. Moving up onto the basement floor, a limited colour palette is implemented into the signage as a contrast to the overall white theme.

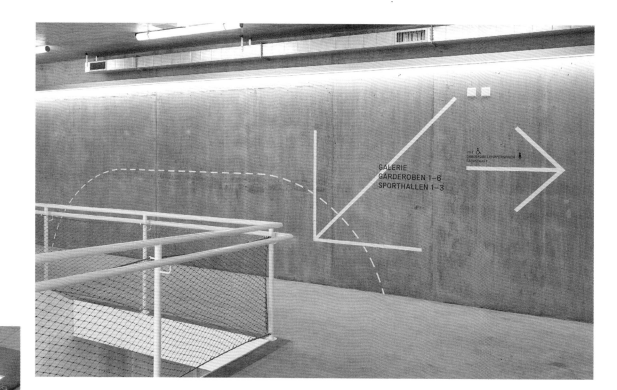

GALERIE
GARDEROBEN 1–6
SPORTHALLEN 1–3

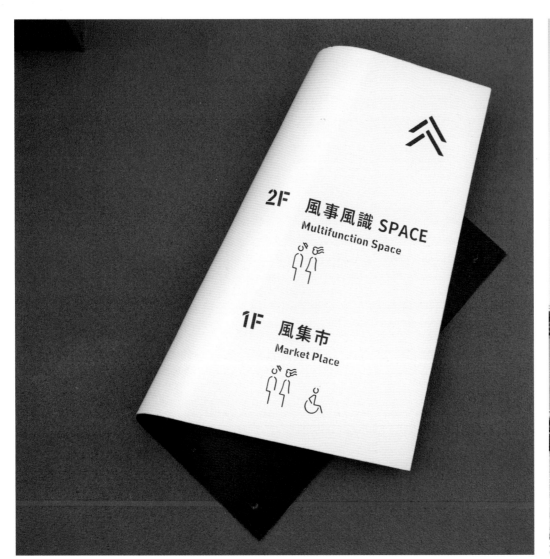

Luo–shan–feng Designated Scenic Areas

DESIGN
Path & Landforms

CLIENT
Pingtung County
Government

ARCHITECTURE
Arch Tenz

INTEGRATION PLAN-
NING
Open United Studio

When the northeast monsoon scales the Central Mountain Range known as Luo–Shan–Feng, its intensity can rival a mild typhoon. The signage of Luo–Shan–Feng Designated Scenic Areas are shaped to appear as distorted pieces of paper that are scattered and blown away by a strong gust, adhering to walls and barely hanging off lamp posts. Conveying the instantaneous speed of the gusts in the area, signposts also feature a distinct graphic pattern that simulates the flow of wind on a map. The pictograms also reveal small 'human' details in the icons with flying hats and windswept hair.

The Luo Shan Feng Recreation Area

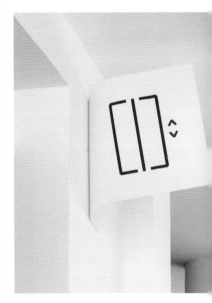

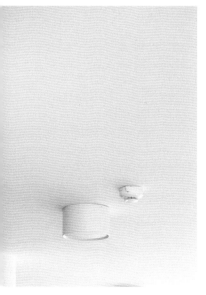

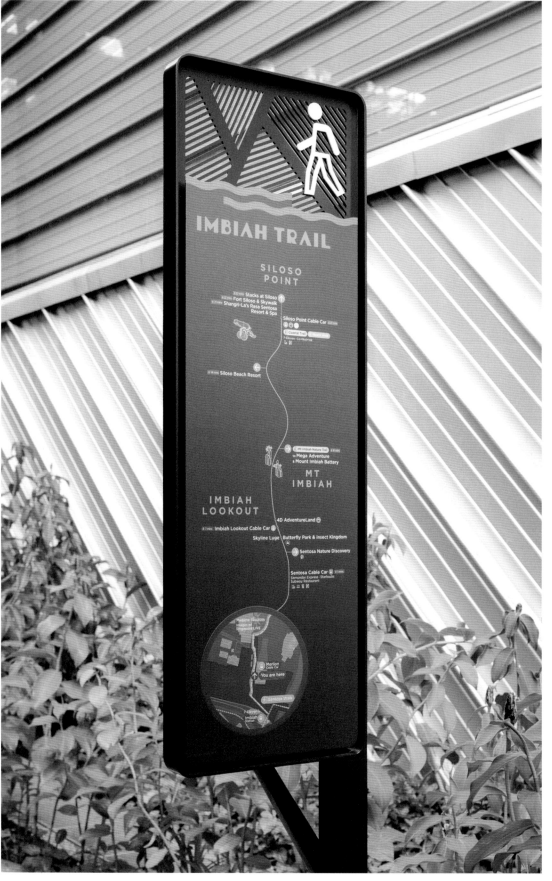

Sentosa Island

DESIGN
Applied Information
Group

CLIENT
Sentosa Is

Despite being a world-class destination, the previous wayfinding system of Sentosa Island was limiting its visitor's experience. Applied Information Group set out to overcome these obstacles by increasing awareness of all offers, activities and locations, highlighting them with vibrant and eye-catching visuals. The new wayfinding system delivers clear accurate information and supports visitors from their arrival throughout their whole visit. The extensive wayfinding sign suite has been designed to integrate vehicular and public transportation, alongside beach and trail signs to promote walking and cycling to allow visitors to move around the island easily.

UA Cinema K11 Art House

DESIGN
Nous

CLIENT
UA Cinema, K11 Art
House

INTERIOR DESIGN
Oft Interiors

With a goal to enhance the experience of cinema-goers and create a warm and cosy atmosphere, the UA Cinema of Hong Kong's K11 Art House's interior design was inspired by the concept of a Swiss Snow Mountain Cabin. To complement the unique theme, Nous established a wayfinding system with the main elements of wood, brass and marble. Large boards were used as substrates for direction signs, adding a touch of modernness with a sleek slab serif font. To increase visibility in the dim hallways, small round signs in the form of an illuminated number plate were hung at the entrance of the respective cinema houses.

What do you like most about designing wayfinding systems? How do they differ from other design practices?

The essence of design practices is to be a tool for innovation and transformation, combining strategic thinking and aesthetics to make information and products more attractive, functional and accessible to all audiences. The passion for building form and interest in interacting with people is the key to the specialisation in designing wayfinding systems. The wayfinding discipline is the perfect intersection between graphic design and architecture, enabling creative solutions that impact people's daily lives. Wayfinding systems are present at various moments of our lives, from a relaxed walk in a public park to stressful situations like in a hospital or airport. The responsibility to guide people effectively when they need information and at the same time create environments that provide safety and comfort is an exciting daily challenge for all wayfinding designers.

● Illustre Ideia Design

Wayfinding is a wonderful combination of human-centred design and architecture. To create a successful programme for a complex place, we need a strategy for how the system will work. Creating that wayfinding strategy is, for us, a fascinating puzzle; what is the hidden logic of a building or campus, what can wayfinding provide, what tools do people need. Developing that framework for the building is just the beginning. Design brings that idea to life, and details ensure that the concept can be realised.

● Two Twelve

For us, the most attractive part of the wayfinding design would be thinking about different objects as a whole and seeing how they affect people's behaviours in the space. Also, wayfinding design acquires multidisciplinary thinking to handle things from two-dimensional to three-dimensional. We develop graphics and layouts similarly to print or digital design fields, but we have more possibilities of playing with materials and textures. On the other hand, only we understand how the architecture or interior (will) look like, and imagine how people will perceive and move in the space, so that the objects we designed would integrate with and speak for the place.

● Path & Landforms

At Semaphore, we love designing systems that improve everyday experiences. Our strategies set out to reduce stress, encourage discovery and improve comprehension of spaces. We love injecting life and energy into what is often considered a highly functional design field. One of our main sources of enjoyment is taking complex and overwhelming environments or processes and distilling them down into an easy and manageable set of steps.

We love working with our wider project teams and understand that collaboration leads to improved and more resilient outcomes. Our design responses are grounded in function and are informed by evidence-based strategies. There is a realness to our work that comes from constant testing, review and refinement throughout the design process, as well as a deep understanding of the broader project interfaces.

● Studio Semaphore

For us, it's the combination of science and creativity that extends across a broad spectrum of design. Wayfinding covers map design, sign design, information design, donor recognition, place-making and landmark creation; no two days are the same and no two projects are the same, each have their own challenges and approaches, and getting under the skin of this is fun.

We enjoy the fact that good wayfinding needs strategic and tactical thinking — what are the key approaches to navigating this space and what should we reveal to people and where should this be?

Creative thinking and the quality of ideas — How should we deliver this information successfully so that it reflects the space, brand or people's identity in a way that is unique and reflective of each space. Watching these creative ideas flourish into robust wayfinding is magical. The best part of designing wayfinding is knowing that you have made a difference to the people who inhabit the spaces — it's about this relationship between people and place and watching trust develop in the wayfinding system.

Designing wayfinding systems is very different to other design practices. When looking at sign design for example, there is a robust rationale around sign design to ensure legibility and readability that sits hand in hand with creativity, and this enables you to look for ways to design signs that push creativity while maintaining the rules. The impact of wayfinding extends beyond the realms of sign design into pre-visit information, mapping, and information design. Designing wayfinding systems employs several district disciplines that utilise different graphical and product design skills.

● Endpoint

While different, wayfinding systems can be combined with multiple specialised subjects such as human engineering, architectural design, interior design, colour schemes, font design, typography and grid systems. A good wayfinding system does not only recreate the character of architecture but also reaches an identical environment, which is the most exciting part of designing wayfinding systems.

● Hand–Heart Design Firm

We have to cooperate with different parties such as interior designers and producers. As graphic designers, we have to understand the theory behind interior design and method of production in order to create a feasible design and avoid problems. It's like having lessons every time when we cooperate with different professions, which also broadens our horizon as we can access knowledge beyond graphic design.

● Nous

We are fascinated by the multidisciplinarity of working with signaletics. On one hand, different design disciplines such as graphic design, architecture and spatial design are merged when developing a wayfinding system. On the other hand, a wide range of technical know-how is required. The end result is correspondingly complex and multi-layered, but in the best case still as simple, easy to read and understand as possible for the users.

● kong. funktion gestaltung

I feel that it is rewarding to systematise sensory forms that express the concept of a place.

Unlike other design practices, I believe that it is important to think about design holistically, as it is a complex combination of many different elements: graphic design, spatial design, product design, lighting design, concept, art…

● hokkyok

Wayfinding is a discipline that's fundamentally about the relationship between people and place. It's easy to say, but wayfinding either works or it doesn't — you'll know pretty quickly if people can't find the toilet or their way out. But wayfinding is more than that. It's about helping people — giving them the confidence to navigate complex places without difficulty or distraction so that they can enjoy the journey as much as the destination.

It's a three-dimensional discipline which requires rigorous strategic logic and articulate clarity combined with beautiful graphic design, elegant product design and precision engineering. You can obsess over arrows and iconography, explore different and fascinating materials and spend days looking through catalogues of mechanical fixings. Like most of design there's never just one way of doing something; there's rarely a wrong answer, just a better solution. But wayfinding can so fundamentally contribute to the character of a place in sometimes almost intangible ways, that there is a surprising power in the humble sign and this is its enduring fascination.

● dn&co

Two main areas come to mind. There tends to be longevity to wayfinding systems which is satisfying as a designer to know what you produce will be around for a long time as opposed to being here today and gone tomorrow. The other thing is the opportunity to get involved with many other disciplines when developing our projects.

Architects, urban designers, researchers, typographers, accessibility consultants, manufacturers, and various other specialist consultants need to collaborate to deliver successful wayfinding. It's always a challenge but hugely satisfying when you manage to coordinate things successfully and deliver the end result.

● Applied Information Group

Compared to other graphic design projects, wayfinding design is larger in scale and longer in the construction process, which requires collaboration in architecture and space. There are many challenges in the implementation of the various materials, which I find most appealing in designing wayfinding systems.

● ONCETUDIO

We believe that designing wayfinding systems is a practice with very unique characteristics. Designing communication suited for a space is different from designing for other media like designing a book or designing a website for example.

There are common concerns (like legibility or the definition of a strong and appealing graphic concept for example) but the space as a design context brings along other concerns related to its own specific nature, that will have impact on the design process. Good Integration with the architecture in terms of colours, materials, or the different scales of the graphics for example are some examples.

We believe the initial stages of the process, when a design concept for the signage system is being defined, are always interesting and very creative moments of the process. The end stages are also very exciting moments of the process, when we actually see the graphics we designed to gain body with the defined materials and colours and being mounted on space. It's really great to see the graphics actually working on space.

What we like more about designing a wayfinding system, is that the end result always turns out to be more than just a wayfinding system. It becomes also something appealing with a unique personality that can create a good experience for the user.

● P 06 studio

For us, it is a discipline that is deeply tangible: our goal is to succeed in enriching both the space and the lives of those who interact with it, which is particularly challenging. In this sense, wayfinding is not so different from any other design practice. It is still a problem-solving exercise, but obviously requires completely different questions and solutions.

● byHAUS

It will remain for a longer period of time than a typical graphic design job. Therefore, it needs to be durable both as a design and as an object, but that is what makes it worthwhile. Signage differs from other designs in that it is large enough to not only catch people's eyes but also affect their physical senses.

● STUDY LLC.

The best part of this practice is being able to actualise a design that makes the most of the building's characteristics and the client's identity.

● Arata Takemoto Design Office Inc.

Information design is a human-centred discipline. Orientation systems are integral to the user experience and the character of a place.

● motasdesign

I think it's fun to think about the balance between the functional beauty of wayfinding, and creating well-designed visual identities. It is also a fun challenge to design in large scales, and seeing designs remain for a long period of time makes me happy.

● ujidesign

We like signage that use certain rules and order; it should always be accessible to all audiences from different backgrounds. Aesthetics come in second place, a slightly different process from other disciplines we practice.

● Folch Studio

At Semaphore, we love designing systems that improve everyday experiences. Our strategies set out to reduce stress, encourage discovery and improve comprehension of spaces. We love injecting life and energy into what is often considered a highly functional design field. One of our main sources of enjoyment is taking complex and overwhelming environments or processes and distilling them down into an easy and manageable set of steps.

We love working with our wider project teams and understand that collaboration leads to improved and more resilient outcomes. Our design responses are grounded in function and are informed by evidence-based strategies. There is a realness to our work that comes from constant testing, review and refinement throughout the design process, as well as a deep understanding of the broader project interfaces.

● Studio Semaphore

Wayfinding combines many disciplines, the main two of which would be graphic design and architectural design. This combination introduces a whole new range of design possibilities compared to classic 2D design. This stands for a more exciting riddle to solve.

● Studio Blisko

Designing signage systems is the most demanding of disciplines. It has a similar complexity to architecture, and a certain poster-like superficiality at the same time.

● büro uebele visuel kommunikation

Wayfinding is an interesting challenge, because people interact with it spatially. Wayfinding design can literally change the course of someone's day and shape their experience of a place. It can also establish a tone for a space very quickly. We wanted our signage to reflect the vibrant community of the space, and quickly let people know that this is neither an outdated historical space nor a corporate conglomerate, but a space that is inherently diverse and ever-changing.

● Smith & Diction

Every new wayfinding project is an opportunity to have fun, because every space is a new challenge that we must discover step by step. We use Design Thinking to understand the problems, needs and behaviour of the user — so our work is a little bit like designing User Experience but in a real, physical space. With our wide range of services, we can make the surroundings more accessible, understandable and user-friendly. We are happy when the spaces around us change for the better.

● Blank Studio

The process of creating a navigation system is interesting because it is not only a design, but much more. It is at the intersection of how to do, where to do and what to do exactly. To create a system, it is important to understand who it works for and what kind of a language to develop for it, so that it is clear and visual, takes into account the requirements of the architecture and brand, as well as creates a product that, with all these introductions, will be useful and aesthetic.

● ZOLOTOgroup

The most difficult and interesting part is to think about systems, especially when it has different varieties and needs. In wayfinding systems, designers should remember that the colour and sizes of words play an important part in legibility. People need to understand immediately where they should go and what they find.

● Orchidea Agency

Sign design is, in a sense, the work of creating scenery. What makes it different from other projects is that it is physical, public and large in scale. It's not a job that can be completed on a computer screen; we have to make minor adjustments in the field.

● Kamimura & Co.

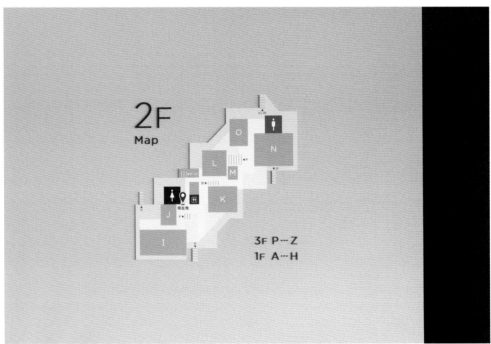

The Learning Station Crosslight

DESIGN
Arata Takemoto
Design Office Inc.

CLIENT
Baiko Gakuin University

ARCHITECTURE
Tetsuo Kobori
Architects

FURNITURE
inter office

PHOTOGRAPHY
Tomooki Kengaku

To celebrate the 50th anniversary of Baiko Gakuin University in Japan, a new building named Learning Station CROSSLIGHT was constructed as a learning space to encourage more communication between students. As a Christian institution, the symbol of the cross was incorporated into the wayfinding, using its intersecting lines to express interaction and guide students in both a physical and metaphorical sense. For the naming and signage for each of the classrooms, the first alphabetic letter is taken from a Biblical keyword followed by the Gospel that it was taken from, creating an atmosphere as if one was walking through a Bible Dictionary.

Gospel — Romans 1:16

U Unity

T Truth — John 8:3

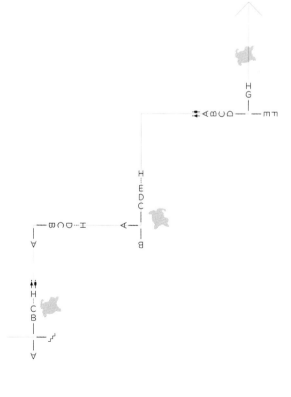

Nasushiobara City Library: MIRURU

DESIGN
6D

CREATIVE DIRECTION
BACH Inc.

CLIENT
Nasushiobara City

ARCHITECTURE
UAo

EQUIPMENT & FACILITY
Kanko, Inc.,
Advertisement Div.

PHOTOGRAPHY
sinca

Newly built in the city of Nasushiobara, MIRURU is a library that also serves as a free, flexible networking space for locals. With a central concept of being 'a place for words', the first floor features a giant, unmissable installation of text from a famous quote that floats vertically across the bookshelves. With the aim to design signboards unrestricted by location or form, direction signs as well as index boards are composed of interlocking chalkboard panels that can be easily carried to another space. In order to accommodate the different events and programmes, librarians can also rewrite the content on the boards and move them around the space.

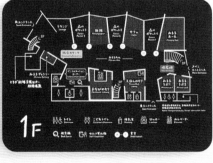

118

Stadtbibliothek Innsbruck

DESIGN
motasdesign

CLIENT
Stadtbibliothek
Innsbruck

In Stadtbibliothek Innsbruck, minimalism and functionality sit at the core of the library's interior and signage design. motasdesign worked closely with architects to design a wayfinding system for Stadbibliothek with the end goal of providing visitors with a clear overview of the library's resources. The focal point of the library's interior points to the curved wooden staircase, therefore the signage was designed to assimilate into the modern interior with a sleek and modern appearance, employing only the use of monochrome black and white while eliminating any visual elements that could be distracting.

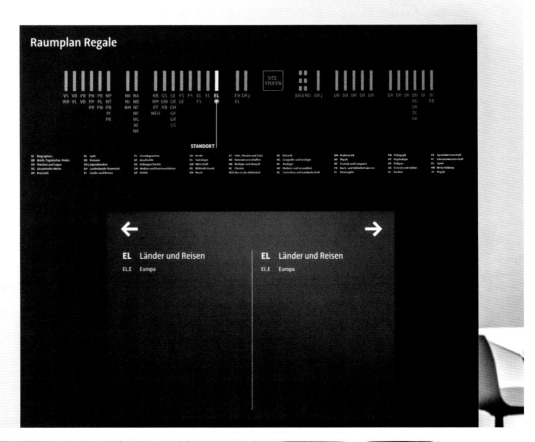

Raumplan Regale

Faculty of Engineering and Information Technology

DESIGN
Studio Semaphore

CLIENT
The University of Melbourne

ARCHITECTURE
Hassell Studio

PHOTOGRAPHY
Studio Semaphore, Tom Blachford

LEAD CONTRACTOR
Lendlease

Developed for the innovators of the future, the new Faculty of Engineering and Information Technology space was built for students at the University of Melbourne. The brief for Studio Semaphore was to create a wayfinding system to showcase the technical, interdisciplinary and future thinking objectives of the Faculty of Engineering and Information Technology, while capturing the consistent voice of the University of Melbourne. The resulting concept used technical and industrial elements, such as the perforated materiality in the storey level indicators, speaking to themes of machining, fabrication and research synergy.

Tennis HQ

DESIGN
Studio Semaphore

CLIENT
Tennis Australia,
Melbourne & Olympic
Parks, Hassell Studio

ARCHITECTURE
Hassell Studio

PHOTOGRAPHY
Square Inch
Photography

Flexibility and customisation are crucial elements in the wayfinding system at Tennis HQ, Melbourne. In alignment with the overarching design principles of the building, the signage design needed to be interchangeable to suit the different modes of operation throughout the year. Each sign in the family has a magnetic face to accommodate temporary signage overlays for use during the Australian Open, while each room sign is also capable of holding paper inserts for temporary notices that are invisible when not in use. These features make the wayfinding system entirely operable by its users.

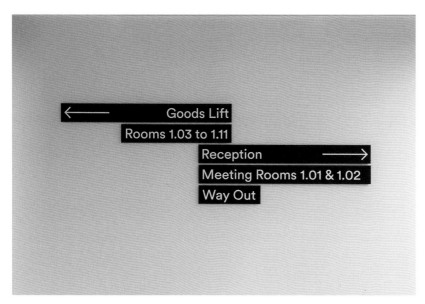

Lifts

5.03

Meeting Room

Do not use lifts
if there is a fire

3   Meeting Rooms 3.01 and 3.02

2   Cafe
     Function Spaces 2.01 to 2.04

1   Reception
     Meeting Rooms 1.01 and 1.02

Shinmai MEDIA GARDN

DESIGN
10 inc.

CLIENT
The Shinano Mainichi
Shimbun

ARCHITECTURE
Toyoo Ito

Aside from housing the office headquarters of Nagoya's local Shinmai newspaper, the Shinmai MEDIA GARDEN also establishes itself as a community square that facilitates arts and cultural exchange, equipped with its own mini shopping centre, spacious event hall and kitchen studio. Using vague outlines and shapes in their simplest form, the signage system adheres to the modern interior, with sleek, narrative pictograms customised to the nuance and atmosphere within the complex.

キッチン

RGF

DESIGN
Kamimura & Co.

CLIENT
RGF Professional
Recruitment Japan

INTERIOR DESIGN
Canuch

As an ode to the people of impact who have contributed towards mankind in their various fields, meeting rooms in the offices of RGF Professional Recruitment Japan features rooms that are not only numbered, but also named after notable figures in history such as Mandela, Kurosawa and Marie Curie. Visitors will also find a short description of each character on each door. To bring a sense of unity to the interior, Kamimura & Co. also created an original typeface with smooth contours and stylish character, inspired by the unique form of the designer chairs used in the office — the Soft Shell chair by Ronan & Erwan Bouroullec.

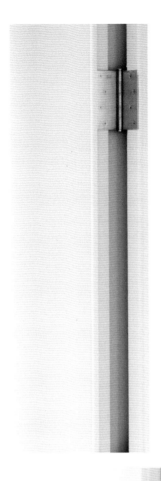

Shakespeare

Pioneering English Playwright.

→〉

Pankhurst

Emmeline Pankhurst, pioneer in helping women achieve the right to vote.

Mandela

Pioneering South African politician.

my CLINIC

DESIGN
6D

CLIENT
my CLINIC

ARCHITECTURE
Soichiro Yagi Design
Office Inc.

CONTRACTOR
NIHON SIGN Co., Ltd.

PHOTOGRAPHY
sinca

Rooted in its community, my CLINIC is an open facility health centre in Saitama that extends to a spacious grass garden and café. While signboards tend to interfere with the space, 6D came up with an alternative solution of using only a single white tube that stems from the ground or wall that is twisted into various icons or numbers. Using colours that evoke tranquility and calmness, 6D's sign plan for my CLINIC features cool shades of blue and grey with minimal use of text, creating a welcoming space for everyone in the community without losing its modern touch.

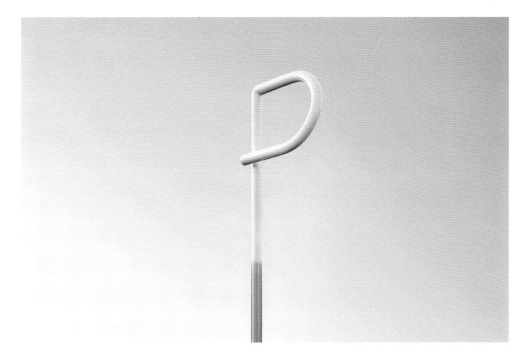

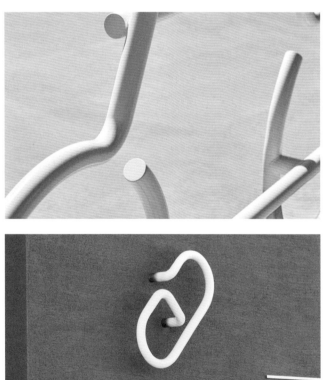

ひまわり薬局

CAFE

138

Ge Hekai Hall

DESIGN
ONCETUDIO

CLIENT
Wenzhou-Kean
University

ARCHITECTURE
Moore Ruble Yudell
Architects & Planners

SIGNAGE MANUFACTURE
Jump Time

Ge Hekai Hall was built for the Michael Graves College of Architecture & Design at Wenzhou-Kean University, a Sino-US institution, where bilingual design is celebrated. A variety of techniques are applied in this project. Notably, lenticular printing was adopted to deliver bilingual messages in an appropriately creative yet legible way. Although the text in English & Chinese overlap, they can be read individually from both the left and right directions without interfering with each other. A series of motion graphic icons also correspond with the wayfinding. The mixed-use materials are meant to be functional but also pleasant.

140

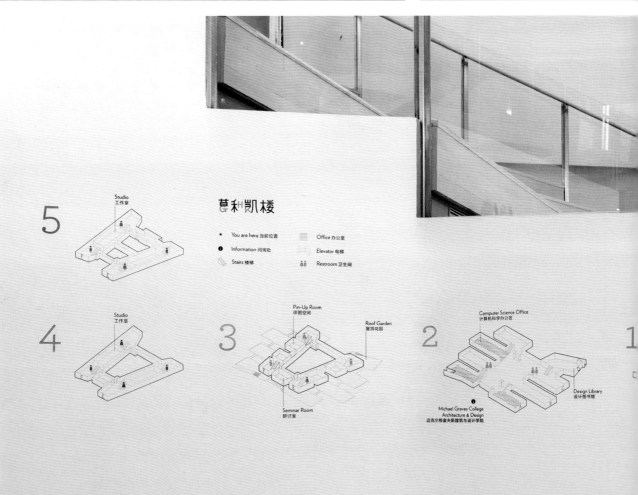

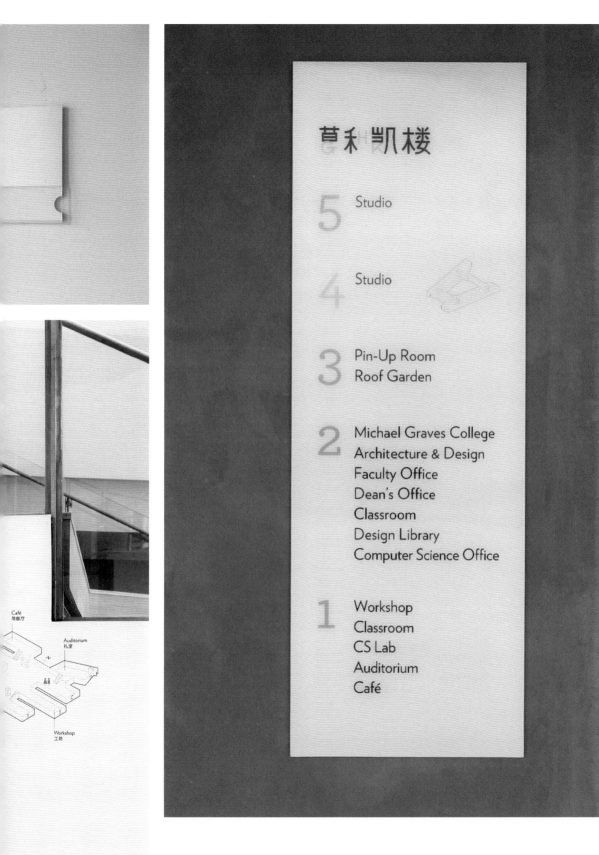

格致凯楼

5 Studio

4 Studio

3 Pin-Up Room
Roof Garden

2 Michael Graves College
Architecture & Design
Faculty Office
Dean's Office
Classroom
Design Library
Computer Science Office

1 Workshop
Classroom
CS Lab
Auditorium
Café

Café
简餐厅

Auditorium
礼堂

Workshop
工坊

The Research Building in NKNU

DESIGN
Hand-Heart Design
Firm

CLIENT
National Kaohsiung
Normal University

CONSTRUCTION
SUNHO

PHOTOGRAPHY
David Wang

PRINTING
Cindy & David
Enterprise Co.

Commissioned by the National Kaohsiung Normal University (NKNU), Hand-Heart Design Firm was tasked with developing a new wayfinding solution for the Research Building in one of the most esteemed universities in Taiwan. The signboards take inspiration from the core element of points to represent the concept of creating infinite possibilities. Each signboard uses a modular perforated metal plate as the base, where the symbols, numbers and text are painstakenly handwoven through the holes with waterproof wax rope. As a result, a unique pictogram design is formed by the joint points that echoes the centre theme of the University.

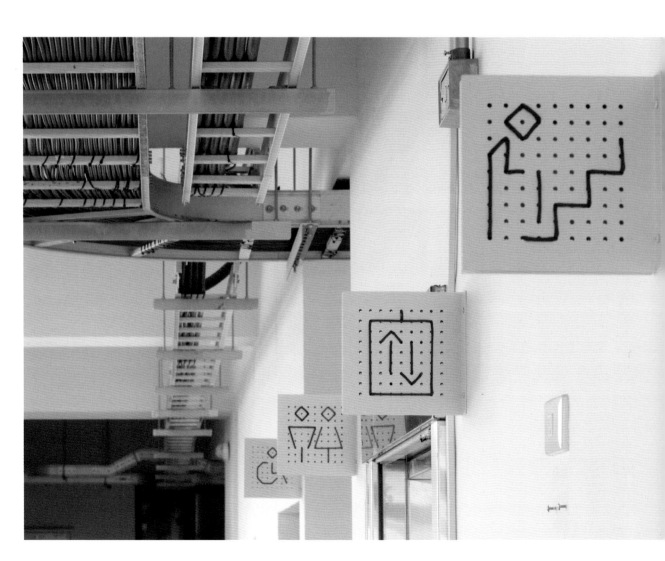

MUNI Nursery

DESIGN
STUDY LLC.

CLIENT
Wajun Fukushi Kai

ARCHITECTURE
Tatsuya Nagao

PHOTOGRAPHY
Nacasa & Partners
Inc.

The presence of light in MUNI Nursery's signage design is inherited from the Buddhist themes of its parent organisation, the Jofukuji temple. The wayfinding of the nursery is characterised by circular, pastel-coloured sheets that slightly overlap with one other, arranged into motifs of flowers, fruits and animals used to identify the names of each classroom. The opaque nature of the sheets also allows sunlight to fall through, illuminating the nursery with different hues depending on the time of day.

2

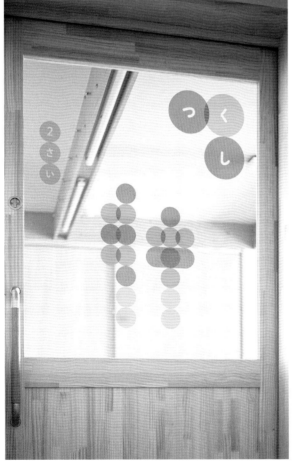

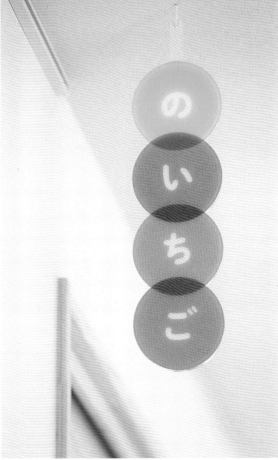

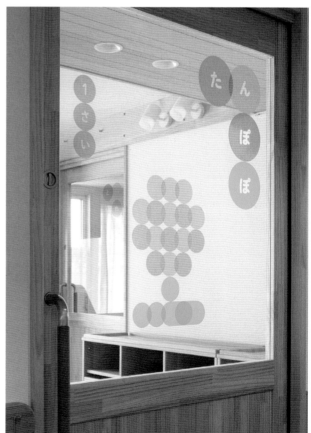

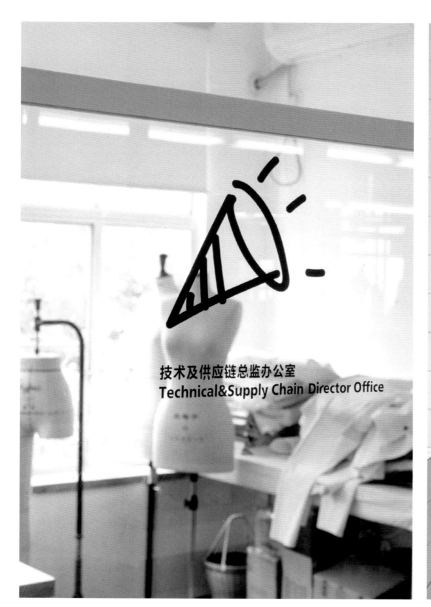

ZUCZUG

DESIGN
702design

CLIENT
ZUCZUG

With life and imagination as its founding concept, Shanghai-based ZUCZUG is a multidimensional fashion platform with a focus on lifestyle, art and design. Headquartered in Shanghai, ZUCZUG's office is positioned as a place for creativity and innovation for its employees, with its minimalistic spatial layout that communicates the theme of "plainness", which translates from the company's Chinese name Su-Ran. Signage within the office space is characterised by cartoonish, tongue-in-cheek illustrations that look as if they were hand-drawn with a felt marker, giving the space a laid-back vibe that resonates with its young and quirky brand.

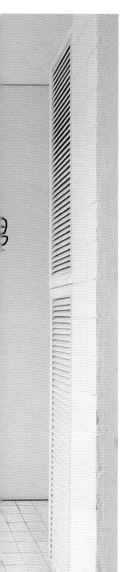

The Software House Office

DESIGN
Blank Studio

CLIENT
The Software House

Rebuilt from the site of an old post office, the headquarters of The Software House in Poland is now a spacious and cosy workplace surrounded by greenery. Establishing itself as a fun and friendly company, the visual identity and signage were designed with black text on plywood to complement the interior design and establish an atmosphere of creativity and innovation. To make developers feel at home, Blank Studio designed a set of icons for each room which are named by the developers themselves. Accompanied by an original typeface, the signboards are built with a sliding plate indicating whether the room is occupied or vacant.

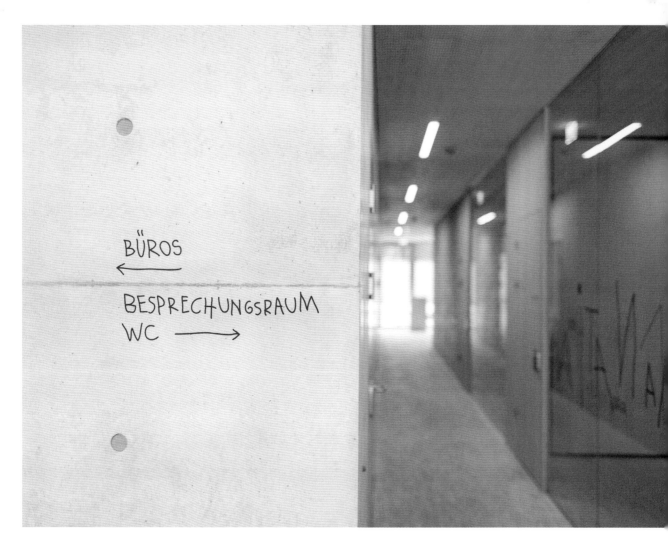

BÜROS ←

BESPRECHUNGSRAUM
WC ——→

Kindergarten Marktstrasse Dornbirn

DESIGN
Sägenvier
DesignKommunikation

CLIENT
Stadt Dornbirn

PHOTOGRAPHY
Darko Todorovic

The pupils of the Kindergarten Marktstrasse Dornbirn were invited to participate in the wayfinding project with their own creations, inspired by the limitless imagination and universe within children's minds. The main components of the guidance system were created and designed by the pupils themselves, with their drawings and lettering adding a warm and lighthearted atmosphere to the campus. The showpiece is the public underground car park, where the columns and walls are designed with thematic illustrations created by the children.

GRUPPEN LIFT
↑
SPEISERAUM
BEWEGUNGSRAUM
WC →

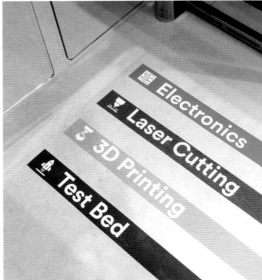

Telstra Creator Space

DESIGN
Studio Semaphore

CLIENT
The University of Melbourne

ARCHITECTURE
Hassell Studio

LEAD CONTRACTOR
Lendlease

With innovation at its centre, the University of Melbourne's new fabrication lab, the Telstra Creator Space, houses various fabrication machines and stations, such as wood and metal shops, the paint room and laser cutting workshops. Connecting all these areas is a system of colour-coded floor markings with graphics that extend vertically to identify each destination at the point of entry. The energetic wayfinding elements aim to boost discovery, experimentation and creation, activate the lab space and create an efficient and straightforward orientation experience for unfamiliar visitors.

ZPSM Nr 1

DESIGN
UVMW

CLIENT
ZPSM nr 1

The new headquarters of the State Music School Complex (ZPSM) is a combination of a 19th-century building that connects the main elementary school building, additional learning spaces and a modern concert hall open to outside guests and visitors. In designing the signage, UVMW broke away from corporate-styled shapes in favour of hand-drawn, user-friendly illustrations in bright appealing colours, making young students feel welcome and highlighting them as the main users of the space. The signage takes the form of flat frames on walls, drawing inspiration from hanging concert bills as a nod to the institution's rich musical history.

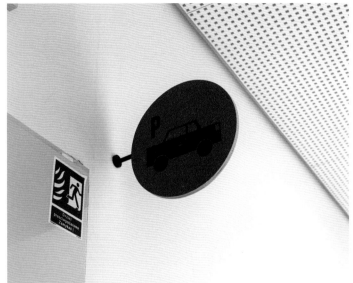

Biblioteca El Molí

DESIGN
pfp, disseny

CLIENT
Àrea Metropolitana
de Barcelona (AMB)

Before it was transformed into a library and municipal complex, Biblioteca El Molí was previously a textile factory with a history that traced back to 1858. After revitalisation, the south façade was refurnished with wide glass windows that invited light into the reading areas, creating a spacious and comfortable reading atmosphere. Respecting the building's architectural heritage, pfp, disseny's signage system used a clear-cut approach that complemented the building's industrial character. Oversized characters are also present in the staircase to denote each storey, allowing visitors to locate their position at a glance.

3
Servei d'informació
{internet i +}
{PuntTIC}
Novel·la. Còmic
Filosofia i religió
Llengua i literatura
Història i societat

i @

2
Informació
{internet i +}
Àrea infantil
Revistes i diaris
Cinema i música
Art i esports
Ciència i tecnologia
Sala 2
Sala d'actes

i @

1
Serveis tècnics
Direcció
Sala 1

0
Informació
Préstec
{internet i +}
Col·lecció local

i

Centrum Południe Offices

DESIGN
Studio Blisko

CLIENT
SKANSKA

ARCHITECTURE
APA Wojciechowski

PHOTOGRAPHY
Anna Nowokuńska

Consisting of five buildings, the Centrum Południe Offices in Poland were designed to put the community and the environment foremost, with a complex including office spaces as well as service and recreational facilities such as canteens, green spaces as well as a basketball court and electric bike charging stations. As a nod to its architectural design, copper is also used as the main colour and element of the wayfinding system, accompanied by an original pictogram that depicts people as the main subject. To increase visibility, perpendicular signage was also used to indicate possibly hidden areas such as toilets, elevators and staircases.

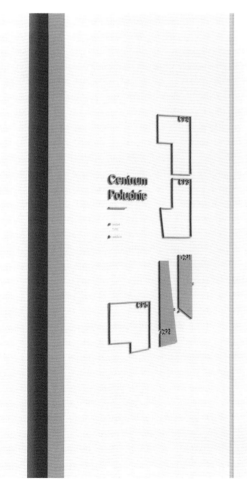

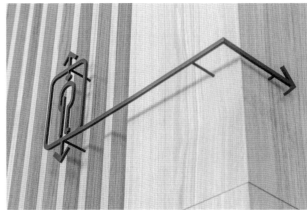

Parking

Zakaz
palenia

CP1

Tędy dojdziesz
do budynku CP1

Citizen Plaza Fukuchiyama

DESIGN
ujidesign

CLIENT
Fukuchiyama City

**DIRECTION &
ARCHITECTURE**
Yasui Architects &
Engineers,Inc.

CONSTRUCTION
Hazama · Yamatora ·
Imai JV

PHOTOGRAPHY
Takumi Ota

With a design concept of a "station–front living room", Citizen Plaza Fukuchiyama was built with an aim to revitalise the central district of Fukuchiyama city. Aside from housing a community centre and extended offices, the complex also houses a library which brings its citizens together in a shared space for learning. With smooth edges and the unique form of a round overhead gate, the signage system and visual identity of Fukuchiyama was created in tandem with the architecture's design elements, as seen in the building's interior and the structure of the bookshelves in the library.

Shimabara City Hall

DESIGN
ujidesign

CLIENT
Shimabara City

ARCHITECTS
AXS SATOW INC. +
INTERMEDIA

CONSTRUCTION
Friends Co., Ltd.
Yamamoto Co., Ltd.

PHOTOGRAPHY
Tetsuya Yashiro

Shimabara is well-known for its traditional craft of cotton weavings that boasts a rustic texture and durable properties, making it the perfect motif for the signage system in Shimabara City Hall. As a symbol of the city, the use of Shimabara cotton gives the space a sense of identity and a familiarity with locals. The striped patterns and dyed indigo hue are central elements that unite the text and pictograms. The sign structure also allows the fabric to be slid out and replaced, a function that brings versatility and flexibility in response to the changing spatial functions and needs of the staff and users.

182

184

2

総合案内

21 税務課
市民税
市民税、軽自動車税
国民健康保険税、税の申告
所得証明書などの諸証明
固定資産評価証明書

22 税務課
収納
税の納付・相談
納税証明

23 税務課
固定資産税
土地、家屋
償却資産

24 **産業政策課**
商工業の振興・金融支援
雇用創出支援
企業誘致

25 **しまばら
ブランド営業課**
特産品認定制度
販路拡大の相談

26 **しまばら
観光おもてなし課**
観光、ジオパーク
観光振興、温泉結婚事業

27 **道路課**
道路の維持管理
道路の占用、用地取得
島原市土地開発公社

28 **都市整備課**
都市計画
公園、建築確認

29 **市営住宅**
都市整備課

会議室2A〜2G
記者クラブ
相談室1・2

3

31 **秘書人事課**
市長及び副市長の秘書
職員採用

市長室
副市長室
第1応接室
第2応接室
庁議室

32 **政策企画課**
新規施設の立案、情報発信
地域の活性化、移住定住
ふるさと創生

議　場
傍聴席

33 **総務課**
市の予算、決算
統計調査、行政管理

34 **市民安全課**
交通安全、防犯
災害対策、防災行政無線

35 **契約管財課**
市有財産の取得・管理・処分
地籍調査

36 **入札・契約・指名願**
契約管財課
市発注の契約

会議室3A・3B
災害対策室
監査委員会
選挙管理委員会
情報公開

議会事務局
正副議長室
第1会議室
第2会議室
議会図書室
議員控室

4

Arup Workplace Melbourne

DESIGN
Studio Ongarato

CLIENT
Arup Workplace
Melbourne

ARCHITECTURE &
INTERIOR
Hassell

PHOTOGRAPHY
Ben Hoskings
(Interior)

Studio Ongarato devised the creative concept of 'Testing Grounds' as a representation of Arup's key capabilities of investigation, discovery and innovation for the comprehensive signage and environmental graphics system. Sitting at the heart of the response is a custom-designed, programmable system of suspended LED signs. Devised to host information controlled by a purpose-built app, the signs guide visitors through the building and orients employees within the activity-based workplace. The dynamic, light-based approach serves to reinforce the technical, agile and open-source qualities of the workplace architecture and the aspiration to put 'Arup on Show'.

LEVEL 2: Service Station
Light Lab, Garden Lounge
Sky Park, Concierge
Arup Cafe by STREAT

LEVEL 1: Arup Eats
Experiential Lab
Bookable Project Zone
Digital Review Space

In our world today, where do you think wayfinding is overlooked and how can it be improved?

The process of navigating the places around us is a vital part of life. There are few places that don't have a navigation system to help you orientate. The issue wayfinding designers have is that as a vital yet invisible discipline it is rarely afforded the same budget as other disciplines; you wouldn't build a building without allowing for furniture or art or not provide an allowance for an interior designer, but often signage and wayfinding budgets are too small or missed out. The impact of this is that it is left to architects, interior designers, or sign manufacturers, none of which specialise in wayfinding.

● Endpoint

Wayfinding is the intersection of architecture and graphics. However, it is often overlooked by clients and commissioned to the construction team without budgets. Therefore, graphic designers should be involved in the conceptual design phase of a public architecture/space project. In design education, it is also important to introduce interdisciplinary collaboration for future designers.

● ONCETUDIO

We believe that it is important for a sign system to be recognisable and to be able to guide everyone, but we also believe that it is good to create a design that blends into the space and the environment, and to create something custom-made rather than something that is pre-made and formatted.

● UMA/design farm

In the case of Japan, there are too many signs, so it does not happen often that people do not notice them. However, in some cases, the information is not organised because it is just written plainly with no consideration of design. Sometimes, the information cancels out each other's functions and it becomes difficult to reach the destination. We think it is important to have a perspective of designing for the entire surrounding environment, and not just the place where the information is displayed.

● Kamimura & Co.

The cinema is a place of entertainment which can accommodate a lot of creativity. Sometimes creativity in cinema signage will be ignored when interior designer only puts all the focus on the practicality of signage. From our perspective as graphic designer, the visual design of signage is also an important part to show the character of the interior. Signage is connected with the interior. Good signage can also leave a special impression for visitors. I think signage design should be considered as a crucial part in interior design.

● Nous

The main deficit in signage continues to be the street. Not in quantity but in quality and effectiveness. We would also say that there is an excess of signage in spaces where it is not necessary. For example, a museum is not an airport or an hospital, and may need another approach to signage design.

● pfp, disseny

We believe a further, more courageous intertwining of architecture, materials and graphics is necessary to drive wayfinding design forward. By playing with space and its underlying restrictions, we work towards unifying these separate facets into a uniquely intuitive new whole.

● Studio Tumpić/Prenc

....

The key is not to over-emphasise on the wayfinding's presence, but also not to overlook it.

● 702design

....

I think it's necessary to think about how wayfinding should exist in a space, and the features that make them stand out easily.

● AFFORDANCE inc.

....

I think there's an untapped opportunity to combine AI and wayfinding. Imagine walking into a space and being guided around one step at a time on your phone — with arrows that appear on the floor or walls ahead of you, guiding you specifically to where you want to go. Why not meet people where they already are, which is on their smartphones? In combination with more traditional physical design elements, AI could open up an entirely new world of opportunities.

● Smith & Diction

Wayfinding is often overlooked in the initial stages of the design process. By not undertaking a detailed wayfinding review in a project's masterplanning or schematic design stages, opportunities for incorporating intuitive wayfinding measures can be lost.

Another element that is often overlooked is the benefit of user testing in real world conditions. Users can offer deep insights into the inherent challenges of spaces that may be missed in site or desktop reviews. Mockup testing, interviews and surveys are a great way to glean information about the successes and failures of any proposed system.

A disconnect between digital technologies and physical wayfinding is also common. While digital technology has become widely used to connect people with buildings and spaces they inhabit, the interface with physical wayfinding is often poorly considered. This can result in the creation of two seemly separate experiences, leading to confusion and frustration. This can be improved through collaboration between the AV/IT and wayfinding teams during the design process, as well a planned strategy for the ongoing content management of both types of assets.

● Studio Semaphore

....

It's hard to say, it all depends on the situation. Badly designed wayfinding systems can be downright dangerous. If in the event of a sudden evacuation of a large facility, for example a football stadium, it can be very problematic and even fatal if the fastest escape route cannot be deduced immediately.

Often, the badly designed wayfinding systems are in places where branding is very intrusive — in shopping centres, amusement parks. The biggest problem is when the design studio focuses too much on the graphic sphere of its work and not on functional solutions. So what if you've drawn cool pictograms when no one can recognise them and distinguish the restroom from the reception? Working on wayfinding is closer to architectural work, than graphic design. With one foot in a solid, challenging design process and the other in architectural workflow, everything you design must become a working prototype. In the end, what you come up with must appear in the space of the object.

● UVMW

....

Usually wayfinding solutions are thought as printed objects or icons, but personally I love the challenge to think about 3D solutions and uncommon materials to make signs unique and interesting for the eye. In a world where we see thousands of images and graphics a day, we have to think about ways to catch the user's attention and make them feel they are in a space where detail and innovation is important. This way, an ordinary sign can become a landmark or even a photo opportunity.

● Mariela Mezquita

Services and entertainment using the VR space are expanding. It will be necessary to guide users in virtual spaces as well. Sign designers have been working with building construction professionals, but they will also need to collaborate with programmers.

● STUDY LLC.

We live in a world where we should be aware of human needs as part of our evolution as a complex society. For that purpose, we believe that accessibility and inclusion must be the top priority in the design planning discussions. Wayfinding is one among many disciplines that play a crucial role in this scenario. To design effectively, we should start by putting ourself in the shoes of others and understanding what matters to improve information, places and services. Through this perspective, design solutions can be created with a different approach and consequently be much more effective.

● Illustre Ideia Design

It's difficult to identify examples of where wayfinding is overlooked. We all have seen spaces or services where we felt wayfinding could have been a bit better and also situations where we felt the wayfinding greatly improved our experience in the space.

Some services or areas of society probably don't acknowledge the importance of a solid wayfinding as a relevant first need, or eventually they do but possibly don't believe the investment is actually worth it and might feel more comfortable in using their available means to make something up.

The good news is that from our experience in the last years, we have been observing a rising trend of people investing in design services to improve their communication and wayfinding as they feel it can produce added value to their business. Healthcare, Hospitality, Culture and Education are probably the areas in which we have felt this rising trend in a more relevant way.

● P 06 studio

Many buildings overlook the importance of signage design while executing the planning procedure, where it is only implemented when the building is almost done. In fact, the design for wayfinding systems should begin at the same time as architectural planning, as factors such as traffic flow, rescue system arrangement, parking lot signs, and barrier-free facilities need to be taken into account. From the view of environmental identity, all signs should follow a consolidated colour scheme, pictogram, typography, and grid system. When designing and integrating the signage, it is essential to realise that those are the key to improve the system.

● Hand–Heart Design Firm

It is important not to forget about a place's heritage and history before working with new forms and structures. This is to respect what is already there instead of destroying the old and erecting something new in its place.

Attention to detail is also very often overlooked. When we work with signage it is important to empathise with the people who will interact with it in the future.

● Tuman Studio

Where we work, wayfinding design is just an emerging industry, and very often it is treated as the last thing to deal with as in a construction project. However, it will be ideal if the wayfinding strategy takes part at the early stage in terms of its potentiality of creating a comfortable and comprehensive spatial experience. For example, the nomenclature of spaces is something a wayfinding system could, or should, work with as a starting point to set up an identity of the place, rather than seeing the system as mere panels with texts on top of it. The user needs of the client, the architectural or interior designs, and the wayfinding system are always functioning at their most when they work together.

● Path & Landforms

Guidance systems are well known because they are everywhere. They have been with us at railway stations, airports, and in hospitals for a long time. Indications, signs, words, arrows, and symbols guide us as safely and clearly as possible through areas, buildings, and structures. But more and more people understand and appreciate the combination of signage with scenography. Beyond guiding and orientation the building becomes perceivable. Corporate identity and exhibition content are conveyed atmospherically.

For years we have been giving presentations on this issue to clients, architects, faculties and specialist institutions. It is important to claim this specialised planning as early as possible in projects. This new understanding allows us to integrate communication, marketing, entertainment as well as information. In all projects we strive for cooperation to find the best solutions together.

● Sägenvier DesignKommunikation

Broadly speaking, wayfinding signage can be categorised into two parts: signs that direct you towards a destination and signs that indicate that you've arrived. Almost all destination signs tell you what you will find at the end of your journey — whether that's a building, a lift, an elephant or an aeroplane. And on the face of it that makes perfect sense; we need to know where we're going and where we've ended up. But one type of sign goes against the flow. More often than not, toilet signs indicate who is allowed to use the space, rather than what you'll find there.

So ubiquitous as to go often unnoticed by the large majority — two or three stylised icons stand in for the huge breadth of human identity and experience. And the issue is; we're not all the same. Perhaps toilet taboo means we don't like talking about human waste or the mechanics of a system we're all intimately familiar with — but the anatomically and sartorially incorrect stick figure doesn't make sense, nor is it inclusive. All-gender toilets have been standard in many places for years — on planes, trains, in our own homes — they're not a new idea. Yet combining male and female icons into a single figure still feels reductionist and ultimately to be missing the point. If we're happy with a coffee cup standing in for a cafe, then shouldn't we also be content with the literal icon of a toilet?

Of course, icons need to be learned and human beings need simplicity. Wayfinding needs to work in high-stress environments and correctly decoding a sign can, at the most extreme, be a case of life or death. But perhaps the solution is to go back to how signs usually operate and show what's behind the door, however squeamish this makes us feel.

● dn&co

As a wayfinding designer, you are always looking for things that either work well or don't wherever you go. Places that you think should have the simple wayfinding principles covered haven't, and they often don't realise the impact that has on the overall experience of a place. This happens all over the world rather than anywhere specific. There is also a lot of poorly executed signage around that feels like a terrible afterthought and doesn't provide the right information in the right place, and therefore doesn't enhance the overall experience of a place in a way it could and should.

A developing understanding and appreciation of the benefits of good wayfinding means we are keeping busy across a variety of sectors and environments. We are always doing a little more than we are asked for in order to raise awareness and educate around what is possible if you approach wayfinding in the right way.

● Applied Information Group

Digital wayfinding systems are an interesting change that could reduce the materials needed to create, however it will be rendered almost useless in the case where power suddenly cuts out, or in emergencies where electricity is used up. Therefore, I believe that the traditional "offline" wayfinding systems made of solid materials are still indispensable in these situations.

● Orchidea Agency

There are many instances where branding and design are overlooked as a driving aspect in wayfinding. It is important to recognise the power and potential of wayfinding beyond practicality within a space, but how it can go on to inform larger systems at work. Wayfinding should be a pursuit of unity between expertise in design, performance and fabrication for the most comprehensive experiences.

● Toby Ng Design

Signage design is not only functional, but also a place to express brand experience and creativity. Therefore, it is necessary to remember that it has a role to enhance the brand value.

● artless Inc.

As we move into a digital world, there is a tendency to think that physical wayfinding will play a less important role in creating legible spaces. However, it is how we combine the physical and digital environments that will create the most effective solutions.

● Cartlidge Levene

Harrods

DESIGN
Endpoint, Pentagram

CLIENT
Harrods

PHOTOGRAPHY
Pentagram

As a world–class luxury department store, Harrods' London flagship store boasts 330 departments within the complex and required a new customer-centric solution to better orient its customers. Endpoint worked with Pentagram Design to construct a simple hall numbering system to allow shoppers to easily find their way to key destinations. From menswear to designer shoes for children, each hall is identified with an illuminated sign and assigned a number, which corresponds to the directions provided on the signposts at the base of each escalator, giving shoppers a sense of assurance with clear indications and improving sales floor efficiency.

↑ HALL I
FASHION LAB

AllSaints
ba&sh
Burberry
Claudie Pierlot
Club Monaco
Elie Tahari
Joseph
Karen Millen
Maje
Meteo by Yves Salomon
Monica Vinader
Pinko
Sandro
Self-Portrait
SET
Shoe Lab
Ted Baker
The Kooples
Weekend Max Mara
Zadig & Voltaire

Atami Bay Resort Korakuen
Aqua Square

DESIGN
hokkyok

CLIENT
Tokyo Dome
Corporation

ARCHITECTURE &
INTERIOR
Takenaka
Corporation

PHOTOGRAPHY
Tomooki Kengaku

Facing the Pacific Ocean, Atami Bay Resort Korakuen Aqua Square is a modern resort hotel that promotes relaxation by bringing its guests closer to the sea wherever they are. The signage design for the guest rooms are also in tune with the resort's central motif, with signboards fashioned into carved and dyed wooden boards that resemble the rolling wave motions and marine blue hue of the ocean, while the width and number of wave steps correspond to the length of information displayed. The materials and colours of certain signboards are also changed to distinguish the guest rooms from other facilities such as spas and public baths.

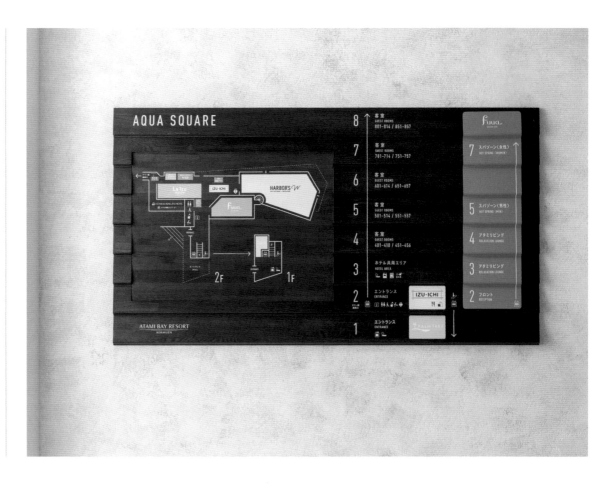

露天立ち湯
STANDING BATH

利用時間 10:00〜22:45

35cm

Meressä

岩盤浴 メレッサ

温度 ℃ 湿度 %

伊豆半島は今よりもはるか南の海で生まれた海底火山の集まり。そんな海底火山の雰囲気と水のゆらぎを感じながら温まることができます。

［効能］新陳代謝の促進・血行促進・老廃物の除去・ストレス軽減が期待できます。

カート
置き場
CART STORAGE
SPACE

ロウリュ キャンプ
Löyly Camp

CUF Hospitals & Clinics

DESIGN
P 06 studio

CLIENT
José de Mello Saúde

PHOTOGRAPHY
José Vicente

In the past, CUF was a network of private hospitals and clinics in Portugal that each had its own image. The challenge for P 06 studio was to create a stronger sense of identity and a universal sign system that connected and resonated throughout the group. The result was a clean graphic language that comprised generous–scale graphics and typography to ensure good legibility and space integration. Partnered with an intuitive colour code and a fully–customised pictogram set, patients, employees and visitors in CUF hospitals and clinics were able to navigate the space more efficiently while in a more comfortable and appealing environment.

Ala
Ward

Saída
Exit

WC

Sala de
Espera
Central
Waiting Room

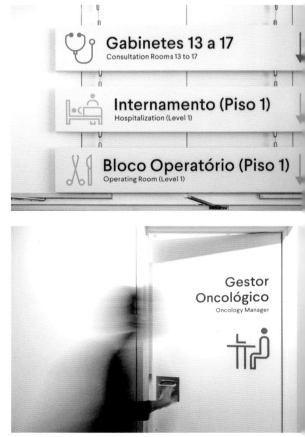

Gabinetes 13 a 17
Consultation Rooms 13 to 17

Internamento (Piso 1)
Hospitalization (Level 1)

Bloco Operatório (Piso 1)
Operating Room (Level 1)

Gestor
Oncológico
Oncology Manager

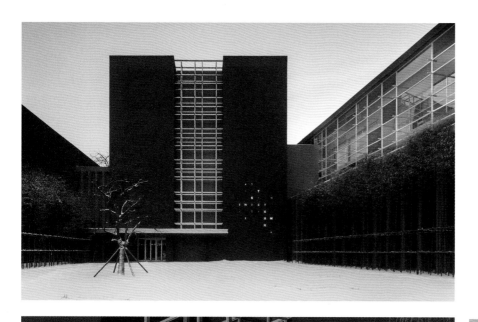

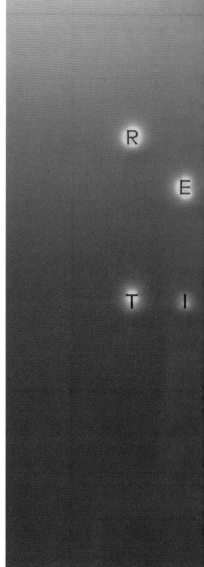

Yanling Jianye Mist Hot Spring Hotel

DESIGN
artless Inc.

CLIENT
Central China Hotel
Management

PHOTOGRAPHY
Wison Tungthunya
(Architecture),
Yuu kawakami
(Signage & item)

Situated in the scenic landscape of Henan, China, the Mist Hot Spring Hotel was conceived from the concepts of "mist" and "colours of the sky", translating these themes in the hotel's iconic facade and interior. By installing tinted windows, light falls through and casts soft pastel hues onto the monochrome building. The shapelessness of mist and the distinct colours of the sky are incorporated into the hotel's logo design characterised by indefinite lines and shapes, while the signage design correspond to its typographic system with minimal lines and calming gradients to make a striking addition to the guest's experience.

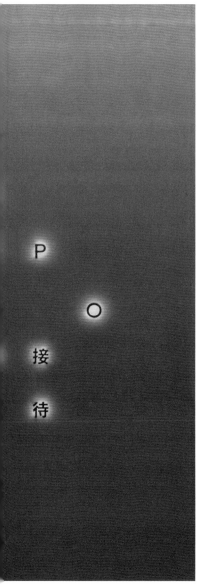

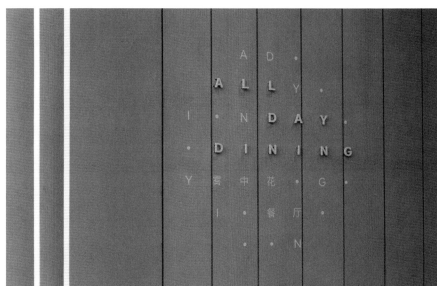

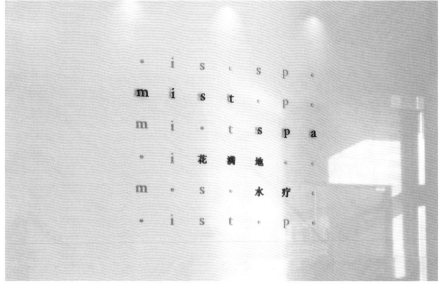

花满地水疗 Mist Spa
健身房 Fitness Room

儿童室 Children Room
水疗书吧 Spa Library

足疗 Foot Massage

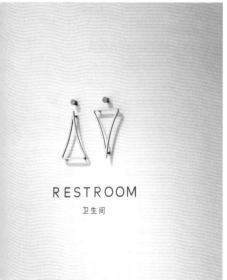

RESTROOM

卫生间

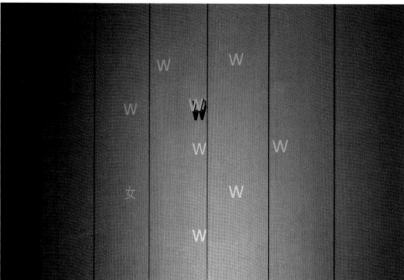

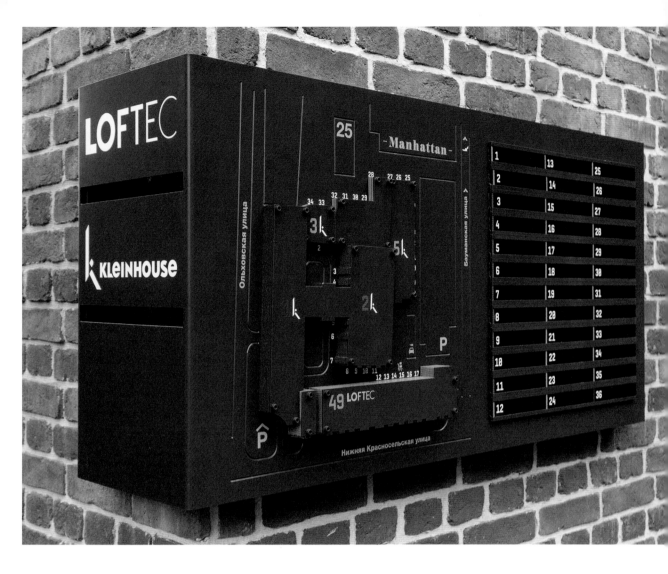

Loftec and Kleinhouse

DESIGN
ZOLOTOgroup

CLIENT
Coldy Group

Loftec and Kleinhouse are two new lofts located in one of the most vibrant districts of Moscow that share a common trait – a rich historical past. Loftec was renovated into a chic, urban complex from a former manufacturing plant with a distinct German architectural style, while Kleinhouse was previously known as a tea packing factory. ZOLOTOgroup was tasked with developing an outdoor navigation system for the quarter where the two lofts are located. The result was a layered interpretation of the building plan in a chic, industrial style signage system that complemented the complex's unique history.

Galera

DESIGN
Mariela Mezquita

CLIENT
Galera

ARCHITECTURE
Alejandro D'acosta

INDUSTRIAL DESIGN
Martina D'acosta

PHOTOGRAPHY
Bógar Adame
Mendoza, Galera
(Architecture)

Built with a restaurant, library, a multi-use venue and co-working space, a versatile signage system was needed in order to guide guests of different purposes around Galera, a cultural centre located in Colonia Doctores, Mexico City. As the centre is open during day and night, white, luminous acrylic boxes have been installed around the premise as an effective signage system that works even without the presence of daylight. The sleek finish of the acrylic and minimal font design act as a stark contrast to the high-textured green walls and disorganised spirit of the architecture.

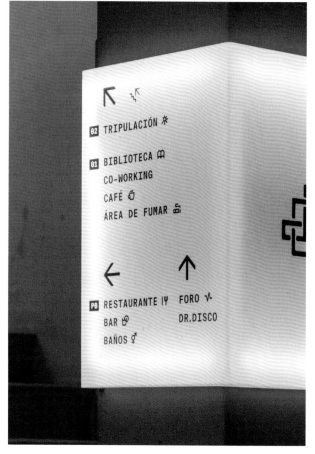

Bikestation

DESIGN
Ilustre Ideia Design

CLIENT
Iguatemi – Market
Place

ARCHITECTURE
Ambidestro

LIGHT DESIGN
Mingrone

PHOTOGRAPHY
Fernando Crescente

Bikestation functions as a multipurpose bicycle parking located in São Paulo, Brazil. An intuitive orientation was first achieved starting with a large bike pictogram on the elevators doors. Interconnected throughout the facility is a continuous white line complemented with text and pictograms, while ground directions act as an intuitive wayfinding system that enhances the experiences of bike owners while navigating the facility. To better identify the bike parking numbers and locate parked bikes with better efficiency, illuminated cubes work as an effective guide to complete the user's wayfinding journey around the built environment.

< grosser saal galerie links   < kleiner saal
grosser saal galerie rechts >
Seminarräume >

Montforthaus Feldkirch

DESIGN
Sägenvier
DesignKommunikation

CLIENT
Montforthaus
Feldkirch GmbH

PHOTOGRAPHY
Darko Todorovic

The Montforthaus is a multifunctional culture and congress centre in Feldkirch, Austria. The wayfinding system were inspired by the winding motions present in the architecture. To communicate the central theme of sound and music, the glass surfaces are decorated with graphic elements that mimic the shape of soundwaves. In creating these unique forms, elements such as music and voices from orchestral concerts and lectures were plugged into software that translates sounds into visible symbols.

parterre links < **ALTSTADTFOYER**

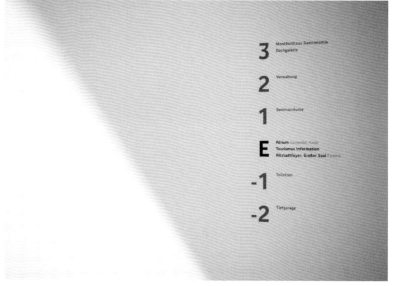

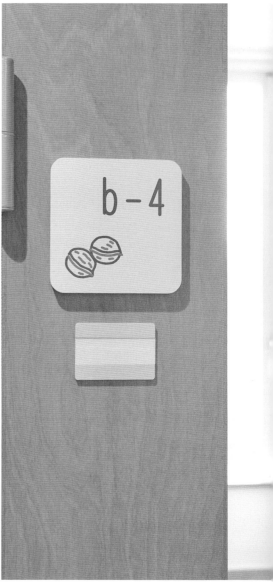

Asaka Hospital

DESIGN
AFFORDANCE inc.

CLIENT
ASAKA HOSPITAL

PHOTOGRAPHY
Koji Honda

The three blocs of Asaka Hospital in Fukushima are separated by nature-inspired motifs of Flower, Light and Forest, with each floor named correspondingly to the bloc's theme. Tasked with redesigning the hospital's wayfinding system, AFFORDANCE inc. introduced a signage plan with a set of icons that feature soft, rounded lines in vivid colours accompanied by an original font akin to a child's blocky handwriting. The blank walls of elevator halls on each floor are also adorned with hand-drawn motifs of plants and animals, amplifying the feeling of warmth and contrasting against the typically sterile and bleak image of medical facilities.

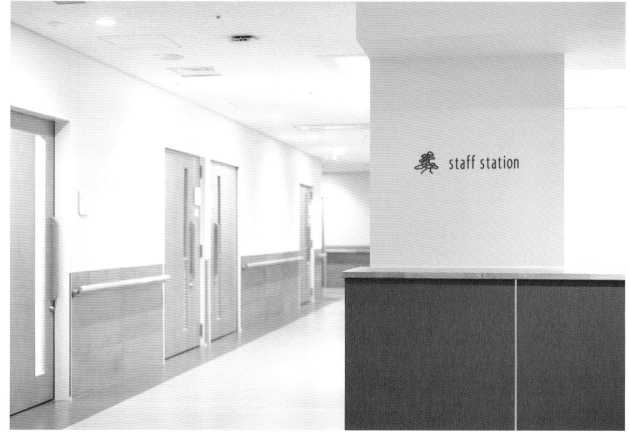

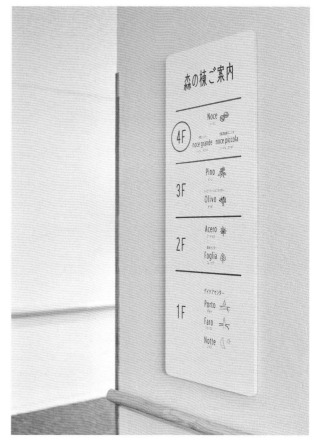

BED & LOCAL SHIBAMATA FU-TEN

DESIGN
UMA/design farm

CLIENT
R.project Inc.

ARCHITECTURE
Open A, Tsukagoshi
Miyashita Sekkei

PHOTOGRAPHY
Yoshiro Masuda

ILLUSTRATION
Yu Fukagawa

Formerly a civil servant's dormitory, BED & LOCAL SHIBAMATA FU-TEN is a hostel located in Shibamata, a district in Tokyo which also shares the same setting of the national classic 60's film 'Fu-ten no Tora'. Inspired by the movie's Showa-era aesthetics, the hostel's visual identity gives guests a taste of nostalgia by combining its modern interior with a touch of retro-inspired elements. To indicate the floor and room number, doors and pillars are marked with unique motifs of parallel lines that indicate the numerals in Japanese characters, while the coloured horizontal bars are reminiscent of the design of traditional Japanese sliding doors.

COMMON ROOM

3

← 307-312   301-306 →

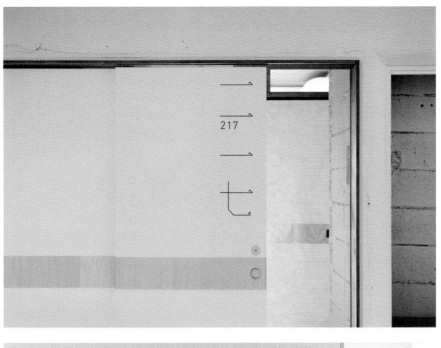

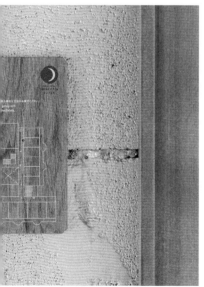

Collins Arch

DESIGN
Studio Ongarato

CLIENT
CBUS

ARCHITECTURE
Woods Bagot, SHoP
Architects

LANDSCAPE
Oculus

PHOTOGRAPHY
Peter Bennetts

Sitting at the heart of Melbourne's Central Business District is Collins Arch, a newly-opened mixed-use civic precinct located on a premier commercial and retail street. The concept of 'Civitas' was established as a cohesive design thematic; recognising the importance of citizenship, a common purpose, and sense of community. The narrative is expressed through all areas of the space with a set of custom-made, supersized cast concrete numerals that reinforce intuitive orientation. Within the commercial and residential towers, a series of extruded and floating wayfinding signage elements add a layer of considered design detail to the interiors.

↑

447 439 433
COLLINS ST

THROUGH TO
WILLIAM ST

←

HOTEL
FLINDERS LN

SMOKE FREE
PRECINCT

Yuen Bettei Daita

DESIGN
artless Inc.

CLIENT
uds ltd.

PHOTOGRAPHY
Yuu Kawakami

Nestled in the quiet residential area in Tokyo's Setagaya ward, Yuen Bettei Daita is an onsen inn conceptualised as a "secluded hideaway in the heart of the city". Created with a desire to blend in with surrounding nature, its sign system is seamlessly integrated with the soft and tranquil overtones of the interior. Directions are expressed by fine-drawn arrow signs with minimal text and symbols, while short stone pillars engraved with directions are scattered around the premises. The pillars appear muted and subtle so as to not disrupt the visual harmony of nature and the inn's Japanese garden-inspired exterior.

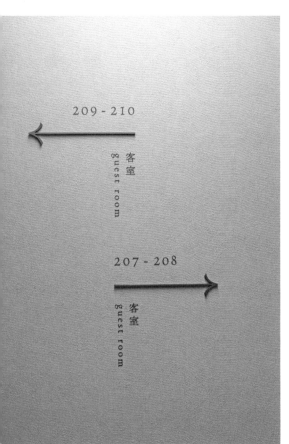

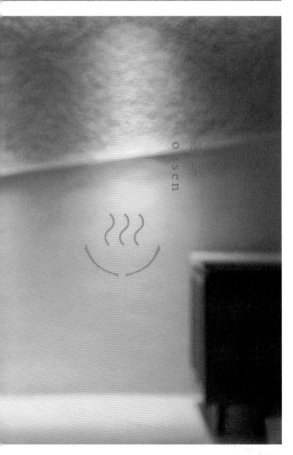

YAN Bookstore

DESIGN
ujidesign, ARTERIOR
Co., LTD.

CLIENT
China Resources Land

ARCHITECTURE
ikg inc.

LIGHT DESIGN
sola associates

Yan Bookstore was built with the concept of "Life in the East." In creating the signage for the grand bookstore, ujidesign installed illuminated cubes inside shelves, placed on tables, and hanging from ceilings, alluding to the form and soft glow of traditional Chinese lanterns. The illuminated signs also provide clear directions in the low-lit, moody lighting of the bookstore without disturbing the atmosphere. At the same time, the rich golden colour of the typography complements the warm hues of the rammed-earth walls, along with the glistening silver of the bookshelves, giving the space a sophisticated and splendid impression.

Featured Studio

motasdesign

Highlight Project

**Skicircus Saalbach
Hinterglemm Leogang
Fieberbrunn**

The Art of Navigating
Natural Wonders

When it comes to human vs. nature, there is often no contest. Although we still have a long way to go in learning how to thrive together better, we are seeing more inspired and ingenious design solutions as technology continues to break new ground and sustainability turns from buzzword to action. Within this context, working with topographic complexities is an ever-interesting exercise in creativity.

One such exercise involves designing a wayfinding system around the sculpted and geologic forms that make up one of the most scenic panoramas of nature and the backdrop for one of the most popular winter activities in the world — skiing. If you have ever stood on the edge of a snowy mountaintop, staring down at powdered slopes marked by pristine pistes, the mammoth nature of the task would immediately become apparent. How were trails plotted when one leafy landmark looked like the next? What's more, how were factors like visibility during bad weather taken into account for the first time?

Investigating the Brief

Spanning over 78sqkm including two valleys and four municipalities, Skicircus Saalbach Hinterglemm Leogang Fieberbrunn is one of the largest ski resorts in the Alps which grew over time through the consolidation of several smaller resorts nearby. Each of these resorts brought its own information system into the mix, generating a complex and unwieldy body of rules and discordant logic that impacted the overall visitor experience. To improve orientation and the sense of safety for all 350,000 of its yearly skiers of different ability levels and nationalities, Skicircus organised a design competition in 2017 as a means to start from scratch.

Amongst all the entries, Austrian full-service agency motasdesign emerged at the top by demonstrating their astute awareness and approach in overhauling the existing information patchwork, which in turn, promised to address the navigational challenges for visitors. These included getting lost, the inability to return to their accommodation before lift and connection closures, fear of bad weather, confusion in times of operating problems, not taking full advantage of the attractions offered due to outdated and often inaccessible information, language barriers, as well as a proliferation of inconsistent signs.

Laying the Groundwork

In setting the foundation for the project, creative director of motasdesign Markus Scheiber and his team worked in close collaboration with Skicircus to define and refine each element in their winning initial concept. The starting conditions and the necessity to completely rebuild the system with few legacy constraints allowed them to rethink every aspect, applying the principles of human-centred design and accessibility at every step.

As such, it was important for the team to have a real sense of place. Besides exploring the entire resort on-ground, systematically and exhaustively documenting and analysing every bit of information present, they studied how effectively design and messaging worked together on every directional sign, slope marking, safety information, digital display and map, in conceptualising and conveying the system of slopes, lifts, regulations, temporary circumstances and topography.

This also allowed the team to focus on hardware inventory and create prototypes for testing and decision-making on certain binary variables down the line, like whether lift entrance portals should be white with dark text or vice versa. Markus explained, "We wanted our solutions to be sustainable, as such, strived to make our system compatible with existing display hardware and IT infrastructure, as well as newer technologies, guaranteeing a consistent design across different technical specifications."

It did not take long for the team to realise that the project's success relied upon the allocation of the most important resource that information designers have at their disposal: the attention of their audience. With too many signs competing with other attention-seeking artefacts, they needed to reorganise and restructure the nomenclature and logic used to reduce the visual noise. Simply put, they sought to present "as much information as necessary, using as few signs as possible" — with legibility at the forefront.

"Beyond the ski slopes and ropeway infrastructure, the main added value to the snow-covered mountains lay in the effective articulation of the chosen conceptual order assigned to the environment. Traditionally, ski resorts not only used their signs as navigational aids, but also as commercial tools to advertise attractions and hospitality infrastructure. The symbiosis between information and advertising needed to be broken for the system to be really improved," Markus elaborated.

Crystallising the Insights

Understanding visitor behaviour was paramount in informing motas-design's subsequent design approach. Working closely with proficient skiers to glean insights about the latter's movements through a resort, how they interpreted signs and what they expected, the team developed visitor personas, their possible journeys and the resulting myriad of touchpoints, which allowed them to prioritise the information visitors need in situ. This led to the conceptualisation of visitor movement flows as a traffic problem, where ski slopes and ropeways were equated to road networks, providing the team with the perfect metaphor to base their design questions upon as they could rely on conventions and widely held knowledge from road literacy.

Through this process, the team also made a valuable discovery, attributable to one of the most ubiquitous ski accessories. In learning that ski goggles vary in performance with regards to colour distortion, they turned their focus to colour discernability. By discovering that the widely available orange goggles create a temporary colour vision deficiency in wearers as opposed to the ones with polarised lenses, they had to ensure that their colour coding palette did not overturn the conventional meaning of certain colours and instead, contain hues that could be sufficiently distinguishable from each other in most weather conditions with most ski goggles.

Approaching the Design

To determine the minimum amount of information needed at any given touchpoint to reach the next one, Markus and his team divided Skicircus into 10 separate zones, so they could organise the information in discrete fragments and progressively present them. According to Markus, this fragmentation allowed the team to visualise the topography in much finer detail and develop a naming strategy that optimised the real estate of each sign while removing language barriers. "We took the 10 main peaks as landmarks around which the various networks of slopes originate, using short labels for each zone (one capital letter from A to L). Then, we assigned alphanumeric codes to the 70 cable cars and lifts, minimising the effort required to navigate the space, regardless of language. This division enabled us to apply a principle of progressive disclosure that effectively reduces the visitor's cognitive load, both in learning the system and in using it."

The team also assigned new, unique numbers to the slopes using a clockwise logic, so the position of any given slope could be deduced quickly. Although this was met with some resistance by operators who already had an intimate knowledge of their facilities, doing away with any source of ambiguity was crucial to the success of the project. Once the strategic decisions of zoning, renumbering and classifying the information according to the type of message were made, the design solutions presented themselves almost-organically as a modular orientation system based on road traffic signage systems. The learned conventions of this internationally understandable graphic language were subsequently applied to Skicircus's signage through type sizes and reading distance, for example, since the average speed of a skier is 44km/h. The layout of the directional signs also ended up being reminiscent of highways or expressways.

In creating the optimal colour palette that could help differentiate various categories of activity and destinations within the site, Markus and his team took on a heuristic approach by grouping colour swatches from different matching systems into colour families and looking at them through ski goggle lenses of different colours and price ranges. Through trial and error, they narrowed down their selection of swatches to those that looked sufficiently different from each other — a process that involved all the pairs of eyes present in the studio looking at the colours in a variety of weather conditions at different times of the day and through a variety of ski goggles in different colours.

248

motasdesign's Key Design Solutions according to Markus

ⓘ "We assigned a specific colour to each category of information in a way that respected winter sports conventions but modernised the hues in order to guarantee good discernibility, contrast and consistency while reducing the risk of less confident skiers finding themselves on a dangerous, difficult slope. The colour yellow is only used for safety information, while for directional signs, the sign background colour corresponds to the difficulty level of the slope indicated. For slope markings, we supplemented conventional colours (blue for easy, red for intermediate, black for difficult) with geometric shapes (circle, square, and hexagon respectively) to remove any ambiguity."

ⓘ "We drew new modern, true-to-life pictograms and user-tested them for clarity. At the same time, safety pictograms were redrawn, so they were harmonious within the system while still respecting winter sports conventions. We also created optical sizes for small uses in print maps and large uses in signs and displays."

① "For typography, we chose a typeface designed to be readable on the move, ensuring maximum legibility even at high speeds. In panoramic map information spots, we kept the artistically painted background of the existing map — an important legacy to the resort — but redrew the information layers with the new system and with higher typographic standards. We also digitally generated views for each zone, where the background representation is congruent with the territory, allowing for more detail without clutter. The panoramic information points include journey decision aids (operating hours, real-time safety information, safety behaviour guidelines and literacy, etc.)."

① "To remove clutter at information-heavy points, such as lift entrance portals where visitors are typically made aware of the rules, risks and legal T&Cs as well as operating hours and connections between resort zones, we created a modular system of entrance portals where each category of information is assigned a specific and consistent position on the portal structure and a specific graphic style with no place for advertising, which was relegated to other surfaces like barriers and enclosures. We also used illustration to highlight the most important safety hazards in a very concrete picture and in context, communicating them in a more vivid and understandable way for visitors to enhance their safety literacy."

Celebrating the Results

For the new system's 2019 winter launch, Markus and his team organised all the production files using geo-positioning software and a clear naming strategy, while supporting the training of employees, fabricators and other partners such as the mountain rescue team. A specially designed brochure was also distributed to visitors and locals to introduce and familiarise them with the changes.

During the first year it was unveiled, Skicircus shared various feedback with the team, most of which exceeded their expectations. The project has since continued to garner a great deal of positive reviews from visitors, resort staff and trade experts alike — winning accolades for setting a new benchmark in ski resort wayfinding and orientation. According to Skiresort.de, Skircircus has "implemented a globally unique piste wayfinding system that is outstanding in terms of orientation, safety and uniformity".

Ultimately, Markus credits a shared vision and dedication from all sides as key to the project's collaborative success. "Designing for a ski park is different from designing for an urban area because of the power of nature itself. The wayfinding system must be very robust against natural phenomena while communicating clearly to visitors about how to behave in the elements. Without proper mainte-nance, the system's effectiveness would erode over time. However, Skicircus is vigilant in this regard, having also trained its employees on how to use the system in the right way. There is always something to solve every day in projects like this, but for Skicircus, a good design team, partners and clients with whom you can discuss openly, made a huge difference."

Mapping the Language of a Walking City

When one thinks about getting around in London, its iconic double-decker buses often come to mind — or even its black taxis, thanks to pop culture. Residents might also see the tube as an indispensable part of life in the city. After all, built in 1863 as a way to reduce street congestion, the London Underground is said to be the oldest under-ground railway in the world.

Although these means of transportation continue to form the main arteries of one of the most popular 'global cities' which received up to 41 million overseas visitors in 2017, it was only in the following year that its mayor Sadiq Khan launched London's first Walking Action Plan, investing up to £2.2 billion to make the streets better for walking and cycling, while improving air quality overall.

Investigating the Brief

In tracing the roots of the Legible London project, this decision was a long time coming. According to Tim Fendley, creative director and designer at Applied Information Group, the amount of walking in central London had been declining from as early as 2005. What's more, for a big and bustling city filled with the promise of interesting discoveries for the curious pedestrian, exploration was limited.

Amid the challenges of an ever-increasing population, overloaded tube system and the growing realisation of a health and environmental crisis, Legible London was born to tackle the perceptions of both Londoners and visitors, in giving them the awareness, confidence and ability to go where they want. Although it likely did not set out with this goal in mind, it has become a seminal project in the history of city wayfinding, bringing together sign typologies, content criteria, information architecture and graphic cues in an innovative way to be seen as the benchmark for many subsequent systems to follow.

Laying the Groundwork

When asked about why legibility was crucial for a modern city like London, Tim looked to the past. "Legibility is crucial for everybody and every place. Cities are actually foreign constructs for homo sapiens. In fact, we were designed to navigate large, open expanses like savannahs, so when we are faced with the labyrinthine complexity of cities, we feel in danger — which reduces our desire to explore significantly. From all the studies we undertook on different city types, including grid patterns in the US, London's medieval and seemingly nonsensical layout is at one time very easy to remember, and the next, very hard to understand. We realised this and designed Legible London to help people learn about the city quickly."

In taking on the project, the team at Applied Information Group — known for its unique spatial experience design practice — had to adopt a slightly different approach. By determining early on that a core principle of Legible London was reliability, or "the feeling the public has when a system is consistent and can be relied on", they focused on achieving it by getting London's organisations to work together. This presented them with their largest challenge, as it involved 32 boroughs, 24 business improvement districts (BIDs), 8 large landowners, high streets, mayor's bodies and transport authorities — just to name a few.

Tim elaborated, "All along, the Legible London concept was about creating a system that everyone can feel a part of and play a part in. We knew how important the project was, how large the task was and the importance of coordination. Although we had an opportunity to apply all our knowledge of different design disciplines in the project, we didn't see it as solely about design."

Crystallising the Insights

To kickstart the project, Tim and his team used a range of research techniques, including interviews, mental mapping exercises, films, audits and group discussions. In the process, they found 36 different pedestrian wayfinding systems in central London alone which were being used only 2% of the time. Furthermore, they found that 44.5% were using the tube map to navigate above ground. Although it was an excellent piece of information design and easy to use, it was not in any way designed for walking nor geographically accurate.

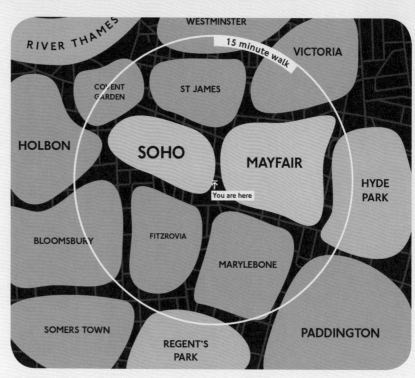

This realisation highlighted the importance of neighbourhood and village names in London. Tim explained, "Mayfair, Soho and Bloomsbury are common parlance. It's often the first way to describe where you live or work. It was fascinating to realise that these names can provide a wide area code for walking short distances: 'Soho is the other side of Mayfair' and yet, there was no official body that determined them. To make use of them in a walking system, we would need to define names and boundaries. We lobbied that Legible London should establish these areas, even when they cross borough boundaries."

At the same time, the team also focused on understanding the different user types and needs. Although this resulted in a huge number of 'personas' being created based on demographics, they were not very helpful to design for — which is why mindsets were used instead: 'striders', 'strollers', people with knowledge of an area and first-timers. Underlining these mindsets was the belief that a good system had to be based on principles.

"If you get the principles right, the design decisions become obvious and their many parts connect. The principles behind Legible London are fundamentally user centric and based on our understanding of cognitive navigation theory. If it doesn't work for the public, then what is the point? In designing this system, we did a lot of work to establish insightful principles and collaborated with a myriad of clients, all with a stake in the project, to help us make better design decisions together," Tim added.

Approaching the Design

As it needed to connect to all of London's transport modes and routes, designing a robust and carefully-crafted system architecture was essential. The Legible London core team composed of information designers, urban planners and transport planners, on top of Tim, Ben Acornley, Simon Hillier and Richard Simón from Applied Information Group as well as Adrian Bell at TfL and Martin Low at Westminster City Council. Product designers Sam Gullam and Dave Fisher, along with a research team from LSE Cities led by Sarah Ichioka, rounded out the multidisciplinary group — a collaboration that enriched the project in many ways.

While the clients' involvement meant that the public's needs and user-centred design stayed at the forefront, the project's tight timeframe also helped to drive momentum. Throughout the design journey, there were many ideas and inputs that were picked, unpicked and adjusted, with personal preferences being pushed aside for research and statistics. At one point, the team even had a big debate about the unit of measurement for displaying distances, as 85% of the pedestrians surveyed had responded in minutes, not miles.

"As designers, we're interested in how people think, how people navigate and how people feel when finding this difficult. We also understand that people only engage with a system designed to help them and one that is obvious as to what it is. Guided by the 'virtue' of design to help engage the public, we spent an enormous amount of time working out how to design maps that would tell a story but not overload minds. All these design skills were married with internal storytelling, so that the many organisations involved could play a part and coordinate among themselves effectively."

As everything had to be tested, trialled and proven to be useful, prototyping was a major part of the design process. A wooden mock-up was created and taken to Regent Street every Friday, each time by different team members, to gather feedback. In doing so, they discovered several design ideas that they felt were ground-breaking but ignored by the public. Initially cast aside, some of these ideas eventually made it back onto the drawing board after testing. For example, the team were keen on removing indexes at first, as they seemed to take up a lot of visual real estate. However, upon observing that around one in 10 people were finding it difficult to locate a street on the map, they decided to keep the indexes to help those in need.

Based on their experience in product design, while the team were aware of the importance of iteration and prototyping, the challenge lay in the scale of designing a reliable city-wide walking system — one that would only really work when it is implemented everywhere without any gaps. Tim cites the tube map as having achieved this, attributing the strength of the system to its consistency because people did not have to give it a second thought. Inspired, the team drew on its characteristics to create and implement their prototype.

"To iterate, we devised a prototype system and implemented 19 signs around Bond Street, removed 44 pieces of street clutter and tested its impact within the small area. 66% of the public interviewed were aware of the system within four weeks and cognitive tests showed a 19% improvement in finding places. This study provided the statistics for successful funding requests to the mayor, leading to more pilots and a wider roll-out. The serious amount of funding this project needed would not have been secured if we could not prove its impact. Ultimately, the results were impressive and delivered everything the project set out to achieve."

Celebrating the Results

According to Tim, the award-winning project's metrics for success were never about impressing stakeholders — but "doing the right thing". As it was measured and analysed at every stage of its implementation, Legible London proved to be highly effective, increasing the number of walkers in London by 5% before the pandemic. By extrapolating the numbers, the team estimate that the system has been used over a billion times a year. Positive feedback from interested members of the public and their peers in design has also been valuable to the team, in recognising their feat as "a seemingly insurmountable goal, a user-centred design standard, a branding exercise and a coordinating initiative — all rolled into one".

However, their work is far from over, with funding continuing to be a hurdle. Although the system was designed to last 100 years, maintenance work and improvements need to be prioritised for optimal effectiveness. Unfortunately, opportunities to commercialise a system like this are typically limited, as advertising would compete with the provisions of the service, making it crucial for its impact to be better measured. Finding ways to do so for a comprehensive system of its size is not easy, but the team continue to work on methods to determine its costs, benefits and impact so that long-term funding can be secured.

At the start of the project, three core strategies were identified: a street system of signs to help with the last mile; integration with other transport modes; and information in one's pocket. While huge strides have been made for the first two pillars, with the system being the most thorough and integrated of any large city in the world, it has not really made it into people's pockets yet. The leap from a governmental system to a smartphone app has not been possible, even though Legible London had a hand in influencing the design of Google Maps. The team hopes that, as the information structure for private systems become more interconnected, the third pillar will slowly be realised.

No matter what the future holds for Legible London, Tim believes that no challenges are insurmountable, as he continues to steer the team forward in other trailblazing wayfinding work. "Don't ever listen to anyone when they say that a problem is too big or complex to fix. With the right vision, drive, ideas and ability, we have an incredible capacity to change things. As I write this, the world's leaders are meeting in Glasgow to 'fix' an even bigger challenge: the climate crisis. We can be confident that it can be done."

→ 10 inc.

Established by Masahiro Kakinoki-hara in 2007, 10 inc. believes that the most important element of design is the connecting and broadening of ideas. 10 inc. has received a number of awards including the New York ADC Award, The One Show Pencil Award, the Tokyo ADC Award,and the GOOD DESIGN Award.

→ 6D

Shogo Kishino is an Art Director and Graphic Designer who has worked in a wide range of fields including graphic design, CI, VI, signage, and package design. With the launch of his own design office 6D in 2007, he has won many design awards from within Japan and abroad.

→ 702design

702design is an experimental visual design institution. It has been fronting the design industry with its signature experimental approach and its vision in innovation.

→ AFFORDANCE inc.

Atsushi Hirano is an associate professor of Tama Art University. His main work includes brand strategy, CI and VI design, industrial design and package design.

→ Applied Information Group

Applied Information Group is a unique spatial experience design practice with studios in London, New York, San Francisco, Montreal and Seoul, which designs systems to make complex places legible. Applied's design has created a benchmark in global wayfinding. Their approach to designing systems goes beyond an operational level and provides complete solutions for everything and everyone that touches the environment.

→ Arata Takemoto Design Office Inc.

Arata Takemoto Design Office Inc. is a design firm active and based in Tokyo. Their work focuses on environmental graphics while they are also active in other various fields of design.

→ artless Inc.

Established in 2000 by Shun Kawakami, the interdisciplinary design and consulting firm works across all media including brand design, visual and corporate identity, advertising, packaging, product, video and motion graphics. The studio has won several international awards including CANNES Gold Lions, NY ADC, D&AD, and the London International Award.

→ Blank Studio

Blank Studio is a multi-award-winning design studio. They are one of the few companies in Europe that specialises exclusively in designing complex wayfinding systems for various public spaces. Their designs have been recognised at many international design competitions such as iF Design Award, European Design Award, German Design Award, Joseph Binder Award, Architizer A+ Award, and many others.

→ büro uebele visuelle kommunikation

büro uebele visuelle kommunikation was founded 1996 by Andreas Uebele. Since 2016 Carolin Himmel-has taken over as the new co-owner and manager. The agency is active in all areas of visual communications, with a focus on visual identity, signage and wayfinding systems and corporate communications. Uebele is a member of Alliance Graphique Internationale and German Communication Designers.

→ byHAUS

byHaus is a studio dedicated to strategic identity design. Through strategy and brand expression, they help ambitious companies to shape their future. Based in Montreal, the award-winning studio is led by Philippe Archontakis and Martin Laliberté, licensed graphic designers. Since 2014, they have been advising small, medium and large companies in expressing themselves on paper, on screen or in space.

→ Cartlidge Levene

Cartlidge Levene is one of the leading wayfinding and signage design studios in the UK. They have designed wayfinding and signage schemes for some of the world's most visited cultural destinations including Tate Modern, The Design Museum, and Westminster Abbey. They work closely with clients and architects to create integrated solutions, and their holistic approach ensures that signage and architecture work together to create intuitive and inspiring visitor experiences.

PP 004–005, 014–021

→ Champions Design

Champions Design is a branding and design agency formerly known as OCD | The Original Champions of Design. For more than a decade, they have crafted meaningful brand strategy and visual identity systems for some of the world's best brands.

PP 078–081

→ dn&co

dn&co is a 100% employee-owned business and a dedicated team of experts specialising in culture and place. They work across six disciplines: strategy, branding, digital, editorial, spatial and wayfinding.

PP 010–013

→ Endpoint

Established in 1999, Endpoint is an award-winning practice, with over 35 talented people across two offices in London and Dubai with a passion for connecting people and place, and to create experiences that make a real difference. Endpoint specialises in wayfinding and the translation of brands within the built environment

PP 022–025, 190–193

→ Folch Studio

Folch Studio designs concepts, brands, narratives, and digital events that reach and engage audiences on a new paradigm.

PP 082–085

→ Hand-Heart Design Firm

Hand-Heart Design Firm aims to make the world better through their idea of design, where "visualising invisible values" is the core of its design conception. "Hand" conveys the idea of being reliable, sincere and friendly, while "Heart" refers to the themes of warmth, kindness and purity.

PP 144–147

→ hokkyok

hokkyok is a Tokyo-based design studio founded in 2015. From planar design to spatial design, the studio focuses not only on graphics, but also on signage, exhibitions, artworks and beyond. They explore design solutions in both 2D and 3D by continuously deciphering the concept of space.

PP 194–197

→ Illustre Ideia Design

Ilustre Ideia is an interdisciplinary design studio, specialising in wayfinding strategy, signage and environmental graphic design. Founded by Rogerio Varela and Tiane Sant'Anna, the studio has 25 years of design practice creating meaningful design solutions to connect people to places.

PP 214–217

→ Kamimura & Co.

Kamimura & Co. is a multidisciplinary design studio focusing on visual identity. Their mission is to shape new cultures today with clients who value the power of design.

PP 134–135

→ kong. funktion gestaltung

The working collective was founded in 1996 by Peter Lüthi, Urs Odermatt and Rémy Allemand. kong. specialises in communication and wayfinding in analogue and digital spaces, developing customised, individualised and unexpected solutions in close cooperation with clients. Besides signage and exhibition graphics, they design classic print products and visual identities as well as interactive and digital applications.

PP 070–077, 096–099

→ Mariela Mezquita

Mariela Mezquita is a graphic designer and art director leading an all female team in Mexico City. She focuses on branding, packaging, editorial and wayfinding design for sustainable and cultural projects.

PP 048–049, 212–213

→ motasdesign

motasdesign investigates the question of what information people need and use when they move around in buildings, nature or urban spaces. As a full-service agency, it offers tailor-made services - from analysis to maintenance.

→ Nous

Nous is a multidisciplinary design studio based in Hong Kong. Focusing on information design, their work includes branding, visual identities design, exhibition design, editorial design and wayfinding signage design.

→ ONCETUDIO

Founder of ONCETUDIO, Yaoyao Huang is an Executive Director/Assistant Professor in the Design School at Wenzhou-Kean University. She received an MFA from the Berlin University of the Arts in 2012, BA from the China Academy of Art in 2009. Her awards include D&AD, Tokyo TDC, CA, Graphis, etc.

→ Orchidea Agency

Orchidea is a branding design agency working with direct-to-consumer brands. They consult, design and support visually-attractive brands that care about the planet and its people.

→ P 06 studio

Active since 2006 and operating from Lisbon, P 06 studio specialises in environmental graphic design and develop wayfinding systems, interior and graphic design, exhibitions, and public installations. With a mission to create memorable experiences that connect people to places, they design using a holistic and experimentalist approach.

→ Path & Landforms

Path & Landforms focuses on exhibitions, wayfinding systems and brand identities. They provide complete visual design and strategy for various spatial and environmental needs, and value the relationships between every single object and where it is placed, in both aspects of the visual experience and information processing.

→ pfp, disseny

pfp, disseny is a design studio based in Barcelona. Founded by Quim Pintó and Montse Fabregat in 1990, the studio works on corporate identity, communication strategy, editorial design, exhibitions, and signage projects.

→ Sägenvier DesignKommunikation

Sägenvier DesignKommunikation is a studio for design communication in Dornbirn around Sigi Ramoser. They are communication-focused designers with heart and mind, as they believe designs are a contribution to culture by combining communicative tasks with function, aesthetics, and independence.

→ Smith & Diction

Smith & Diction is a branding and design studio in Philadelphia. They specialise in making thoughtful identities for imaginative clients, only take on projects they're excited about, and treat every client like a big one. Their portfolio includes visual identities, packaging, wayfinding, copywriting, and editorial design.

→ Studio Blisko

Studio Blisko combines graphics with architecture to create wayfinding systems. Knowing the specifics of the architectural industry and the stages of the design process, the studio creates clear and unique solutions, while always referring to the look and feel of architecture, the main idea of the design, and function.

→ Studio Ongarato

For 25 years, Studio Ongarato has challenged the conventions of branding, wayfinding and placemaking through strategic interrogation of brand and context.

→ Studio Semaphore

Studio Semaphore is a wayfinding signage design firm based in Melbourne, with a team of experienced wayfinding specialists providing strategy-lead creative outcomes to improve navigation and understanding of complex sites. The studio has established its position as recognised experts at the forefront of wayfinding design with a refined delivery methodology and collaborative approach.

PP 122–129, 164–165

→ Studio Tumpić/Prenc

Founded by Anselmo Tumpić, Studio Tumpić/Prenc works on a variety of interesting projects ranging from marketing campaigns, identity and packaging designs, to interactive exhibitions. The work of Studio Tumpić/Prenc has received recognition from industry leaders such as Red Dot Best of the Best, European Design Award Best on Show, IIID Award, Communication Art Award, ADC Europa and Epica.

PP 092–095

→ Study LLC.

STUDY LLC. was founded by Takahiro Eto in 2016. Born in Shizuoka, Eto graduated from the Graduate School of Tama Art University (Ph.D.) in 2010 and set up STUDY LLC. in Tokyo where he works now. He enjoys experimenting with specific expressions and creating graphic design in various fields.

PP 090–091, 148–151

→ Toby Ng Design

Toby Ng Design is an award-winning independent branding and design studio based out of Hong Kong. Formed by the practice of distilling ideas to their essence, they work through the clutter to communicate with value and substance for effective solutions that support significant ideas.

PP 050–053

→ Tuman studio

Based in Moscow and operating internationally, Tuman studio is a graphic design studio specialising in brand identities, cultural and environmental design founded by Ira Kosheleva and Costa Tol.

PP 046–047

→ Two Twelve

Two Twelve is a group of public information designers who specialise in wayfinding, signage design, and presenting complicated information in a simple way. Based in NYC and Honolulu, they work on projects around the world. Two Twelve are experts in developing strategic plans that make information and environments easier to navigate, and have deep roots in wayfinding, signage design, and environmental graphic design.

PP 026–029

→ ujidesign

Founded in 2005 by Yutaka Maeda, ujidesign's services include graphics, sign design, package design, book design and web design.

PP 058–061, 178–185, 238–240

→ UMA/design farm

UMA/design farm was founded in 2007 by art director and designer Yuma Harada in Osaka. 7 members, led by him, are currently involved in total design, including graphics, signage, packaging, brand identity, and planning, and are practicing design through repeated dialogue and experimentation.

PP 030–033, 062–065, 226–229

→ UVMW

UVMW is a team of designers who specialise in creating unusual branding and visual communication projects. Developing lots of creative solutions for cultural and business issues, they realise many untypical branding tasks, from small forms to big identification systems and multichannel advertising campaigns.

PP 166–169

→ ZOLOTOgroup

ZOLOTOgroup is an interdisciplinary team engaged in a variety of projects in the areas of territorial development, branding, navigation systems, and visual brand communication strategies. Their projects focus on the individual and their user experience while responding to the needs of customers in a way that increases visitor numbers, profit and brand awareness.

PP 208–211

Acknowledgement

We would like to thank all the designers and companies who were involved in the production of this book. This project would not have been accomplished without their significant contribution to its compilation. We would also like to express our gratitude to all the producers for their invaluable opinions and assistance throughout this entire project. Its successful completion owes a great deal to many professionals in the creative industry who have given us precious insights and comments. And to the many others whose names are not credited but have made specific input in this book, we thank you for your continuous support the whole time.

Future Editions

If you wish to participate in viction:ary's future projects and publications, please send your website or portfolio to submit@victionary.com